The Last Word On
LEFSE

The Last Word On
LEFSE

Gary Legwold

Adventure Publications

CAMBRIDGE, MINNESOTA

THE LAST WORD ON LEFSE
© 1992 by Gary Legwold

Published by
Adventure Publications, Inc.
P.O. Box 269
Cambridge, MN 55008
1-800-678-7006

ISBN 0-934860-78-5

COVER PHOTOGRAPH BY CHRIS FAUST

All photos by Gary Legwold unless otherwise credited.
Photos repeated in recipe section credited where they first appear.

The following lyrics and poems used with permission of their authors:
p. 47, poem from the *Centennial Cook Book* by the Lutheran Church Wom-
en of Starbuck; p. 120, "The Lefse Song" from Red Stangland's *Norwegian
Home Companion*; p. 151, poem from *Cream and Bread* by Janet Martin and
Allen Todnem; p. 160, "Oh Ya You Betcha" and "Deck the Halls" from
91 Ways To Serve Lefse by Merlin Hoiness; p. 167, "I'll Be Home For
Lefse" by LeRoy Larson; p. 168, "Just A Little Lefse Will Go A
Long Way" by Stan Boreson and Doug Setterberg.

To Grandma and sister Mary,
But most of all to Jane,
Who has eaten my worst lefse,
And my best.

Acknowledgments

Thanks to Lisa Jenison, who searched high and low in libraries for information on lefse. To Virginia See and Kathy Erickson, who, while at The Lazear Agency in Minneapolis, were extremely helpful in getting the book going.

To Stu Abraham and Don Leeper, who saw possibilities in this lefse book and challenged me to write it. To Don Leeper's grandmother-in-law, Mrs. Mabel Schusted, for appearing on the cover.

To the folks at Vesterheim, the Norwegian-American Museum in Decorah, Iowa, and to the good people at the Sons of Norway, for their assistance in finding fabled lefse makers.

To Hazel Retzlaff, who edited the manuscript with skill and respect.

To Reg Sandland, who laid out the book with style and creativity.

To the other members of The Buckaroos—Cris Anderson, Tom Eckstein, and Earl Hipp—who, over breakfast every other Thursday, offered support and feedback.

Finally, thanks to all the wonderful lefse makers I met. Keep on rolling.

Contents

The Last Word On
LEFSE

1
For the Love
of Lefse

I LOVE LEFSE. That is why I wrote this book. For me, it wasn't enough to learn how to make lefse and eat it at holidays. I found lefse fascinating stuff and had to learn everything I could about it: the recipes, the lefse-making techniques, the corny songs and poems and jokes, the lovely people who make it, and the culture and stories behind it.

Lefse, before this book, represented a rather frayed lifeline to my Scandinavian heritage. I didn't know Norske from Nottingham, but I knew Grandma Legwold made something Norwegian that I ate as a kid: lefse.

I'm only beginning to know Norwegian and Norwegian-American ways, but at least I'm on my way in a journey that helps define who I am. And the thanks for getting me started goes to lefse. The way back to Norway is through my stomach.

I confess that this book is, in no small way, nostalgia, Norwegian-style. I challenged the scores of lefse makers I interviewed to look back and then tell me what lefse meant to them and their families, especially at the holidays. Why was lefse so important? What they said is what you'll read.

Nothing warms a kitchen as much as making lefse. Our two little ones, three-year-old Kate and six-year-old Ben, guided Jane and I through this part of making lefse dough. Ben grimaced as he showed how ricing potatoes can be done with gusto.

With nostalgia, of course, often comes excessive sentiment, a wistful, uncritical yearning for the good old days. I've tried my best to tone this kind of mush down, but at times I have failed miserably. I have become a man who, at age forty-one, has begun to fall in love with his people and their ways. In my defense I will say this: You sit and talk lefse and life for hours in the peaceful little kitchen of eighty-two-year-old Sabel Jorde (they don't make names as beautiful as that any more,) and then not get a little sentimental about the past. Things sure seemed simpler in Sabel's salad days.

I confess, too, that in my sentimental journey I have idealized lefse makers. I admit I was not looking for warts when I visited lefse makers and heard their stories. Sure, I found flaws, but for the most part I found people who could be my neighbor any day. I would never have to lock my door, and I know theirs would always be open to me.

I was looking for—and I found—inspiration and humor from lefse makers. I was biased, though, an easy mark. Other people may have been non-plussed by my lefse discoveries, but I was "romancing the round," so to speak. I wanted Ida Sacquitne, The Grand Ol' Lady of Lefse, to awe me. And she did. To others she may have been just another little old lady. To me she was Ida the Great.

I wanted Carl Knutson to dazzle me with the lefse songs he wrote on the roads of Minnesota, North Dakota, and Montana—back when he was selling lefse out of the back seat of his '47 Chevy. And he did.

I wanted The Boys of Starbuck to spellbind me with the tale of how they made The World's Largest Lefse one hot July day on the shores of Lake Minnewaska. And they did.

I wanted Herb Solum to recover enough from his stroke so that he and Anna could make lefse again at Christmas. And he did.

I wanted to be mesmerized by Bitten and Torbjorn Norvoll's accounts about lefse in the old country and of their experiences during World War II, when Norway had been occupied. And I was.

I wanted to hear silly things about lefse, like how Anna Alden used to make lefse on roller skates. Or how the public health inspector caught grocer Merlin Hoiness "bootlegging" lefse, to use his word. Or how if a newcomer to Kathy Weflen's family didn't come to like lefse eventually, then that person's taste, certainly—and perhaps character—was under suspicion. I wanted to hear such silly things. And I did.

The heart of *The Last Word on Lefse* came from the hearts of lefse makers who had a tale to tell and a lefse round, plus coffee, to share. Sure, the book has recipes, which are in the easy-to-find blonde-paged section at the end of the book. There is also a how-to-make-lefse section that includes some of the best tips I picked up from some of the best lefse makers. There is even a Christmas lefse skit you can read—or perform—at your next Christmas gathering.

But this book is not so much a tribute to lefse itself as it is to the folks who make it, especially the older ones, the grandmas. Lefse making keeps them in demand, busy, vital. Their phones keep ringing, particularly come Christmastime. They have no time for talk of withering on the vine. There's a saying:

> When you're green, you grow,
> And when you're ripe, you rot.

Lefse makers, if you look closely under all that flour, stay green.

2
Elusive Lefse

MY FIRST BATCH of lefse had crunch to it. It was a dry, kind of crinkly parchment, not even close to the soft and sprawling lefse doilies Grandma Legwold used to make. Those membrane-thin masterpieces hissed on the grill, then bubbled and steamed and browned, with little liver spots like those on the backs of Grandma's aging but agile hands.

No, an unbiased observer would take one look at my first lefse, remove his hat solemnly, and say, "Save your sugar, son; don't even bother rolling it."

Of course I did roll it one pre-holiday night years ago, more out of curiosity and conceit than because of any appetite for this dusty "delicacy" before me. Whew, the stuff was tough. You couldn't nibble your way to the end of the roll, as with real lefse. You had to sink your incisors into the roll, yank, and hope to heavens the choppers would hold. To call it lefse was way wide of the mark. This was potato jerky. You could tie a couple knots at the ends of this lefse, and pitch it to your teething puppy.

When I swallowed the truth about my lefse, I was a shaken man. Such expectations I had had when I bought a Bethany sixteen-inch electric lefse grill, a grooved rolling

*Lefse started for me with Grandma Jennie Legwold, pictured here
with Grandpa Carl on their fiftieth wedding anniversary. She'd
make soft and sprawling lefse doilies for the times I'd
visit her and Grandpa in Peterson, Minnesota.*

pin, and two twenty-four-inch birch lefse sticks with beveled
tips. I love lefse. I love its taste, its smell, its look, and its
velvet floury feel. That feel reminds me of Grandma Jennie
Legwold's slightly-powdered cheek, a cheek I'd kiss when I'd
go to Peterson, Minnesota, to visit her and Grandpa Carl.

Grandma was a lot like lefse, I suppose: There was nothing about either to dislike, and plenty to love. Just as pota-

toes and lefse seemed to be always on the table and always warm, so was Grandma: always there and always warm to every member of the family. I think for many of us Scandinavians, lefse is ultimately about Grandmas.

Anyway, I had bought lefse-making tools because I love lefse, and no one in the family seemed to be making it. In fact, no one in my generation or my parents' generation seemed to be making it. We were either intimidated ("Oh, I could never make it like Grandma's,") or we didn't seem to give a holy hoot. We either bought a package or two for the holidays, or we left the lefse labor to our proud grandparents.

Now I know that's not true—lots of people make lefse—but back then I had just moved to Minnesota from Illinois, where people don't know lefse from lutefisk. And the sobering question remained: Who would be left to make lefse if my generation abandoned the art?

Well, I had taken action and failed miserably. Now what? Was the Scandinavian stock in my family indeed weakening? What I wouldn't have given for a lefse hotline; I needed help, specific technique tips. And I needed someone to tell me, "You are not your lefse."

I tried making lefse again the next year. Same sad results. I learned the expression *uff da*, Norwegian for "Oh my." I had heard that too much flour meant tough dry lefse, but, heck, unless I *showered* my dough repeatedly with flour, there was no way I could roll the stuff without it sticking to my regular pie-crust rolling pin and Tupperware mat.

I tried blowing off excess flour before I put the lefse on the grill. I'd pick up this precious rolled-out lefse that, miracle of miracles, did not stick or tear, and move reverently to the sink. I'd blow off a cloud of flour, open my eyes to make sure the gust had not tattered my potato baby, then set it on the grill and wait for life in those wondrous bubbles that billow up as the lefse bakes.

Shoot, I might as well have thrown a dusty dishcloth on the grill. There were no bubbles, and my kitchen looked like it had been whitewashed. On contact, my apron and shirt poofed with flour, and my hair and eyelashes were white. I was one angry albino. *Fy da* (for shame.) I couldn't face lefse making again. I'd been beaten. After that, I'd say I was too busy for lefse making, or I'd buy it and complain that "this wasn't so good."

Then one year my cousin's wife, Linda Bengtson, gave away a tin of lefse at our Christmas gathering. I nonchalantly asked to see the tin; it was like opening a magic box. There they were. Lefse, thin and blonde and pliant, folded into triangles and stacked neatly.

"You made this?" I said with wonderment. My fingers touched the top triangle, and I studied its surface the way an art student studies a Kroyer.

It took restraint not to throw myself at Linda's feet and beg her to show me—right then and there—how to do this. Instead, I began serving my lefse-making apprenticeship. She gave me tips, a different recipe, and a smaller rolling pin made by Lars Hjermstad in Wanamingo, Minnesota, where she lived. She also became my lefse therapist, so to speak, assuring me I'd get it and that, really, lefse was just lefse. Nothing more or less.

I was making progress, but the lefse was still a little on the tough side. When I called Linda and did a little whining, she went down her list of troubleshooting questions, then finally said, "Gee, I don't know what it could be. What kind of pastry cloth do you use?"

"Pastry cloth? What's a pastry cloth?" I said, but I knew a big piece of the puzzle had just fallen in place. I was using a Tupperware mat and my lefse dough was sticking. So I had to add flour, which made for thick, tough lefse. With the cotton-polyester pastry cloth, there was less sticking especially when flour got worked into the fabric. I tried the pastry cloth and at long last: thin lefse.

I felt I had arrived, that a good batch of lefse was no longer elusive, although my "rounds" were (and are) more ragged at the edges than round. Still, I was more than curious about lefse. Yeah, lefse. There was something about it—the people making it, the culture behind it, the holiday associations, who knows what else—that lured me. I knew that lefse making settled me down, lightened me up, smoothed out my rough edges, and invariably stirred up heartwarming memories. Did it do the same for others? If so, why? What was it about lefse, of all things, that spoke so strongly to the heart and soul—and stomach?

As I sought answers to these questions from legendary lefse makers, usually living in small Norwegian-American towns in the Upper Midwest, I realized that in a way I was on a somewhat silly search for oracles named Ole and Lena, mortals through whom a deity was believed to speak as they rolled out a few rounds of lefse.

I can now say that I did not find oracles, just good friendly folks who offered me a tip or two about lefse. But as they did that, they also passed on to me glimpses of their families, their humor, occasionally their hurt, their heritage, and their holidays. Which is to say that they caused me to look again at my family, my humor, occasionally my hurt, my heritage, my holidays—myself. These were steady, solid, unpretentious people who just kept rolling through the years. They may not have known exactly where they were going in life, but they usually had a pretty good idea. At the very least, they knew where they were from—and had never forgotten it. Lefse making was just one way they showed it.

Dennis Jacobs would be the first to tell you he's no oracle. The day I visited him he was simply head honcho at The House of Jacobs, a lefse-making firm in Spicer, Minnesota. Jacobs once lived in Milwaukee and plugged away at accounting for thirteen years, long enough to realize he was "fed up with that kind of work." (He must have been, because he hired an accountant to do his books.)

He came back home with a lefse business in mind. His mother, Bernice Jacobs, had come from a Scotch, Irish, and German background and hadn't made lefse until about fifteen years before when husband John, a Norwegian, started dropping heavy hints that enough was enough, he wanted homemade lefse.

So Bernice made lefse but had a devil of a time because the dough was sticking to the counter as she rolled her rounds. John made a twenty-three-and-a-half-inch round pastry board with a cotton-polyester cover. That took care of the sticking. Bernice could now roll with the best of them, and John was one happy guy.

Word got out about this pastry board and cover, and soon Bernice and John were in a magazine article and at craft shows, apologizing because they had run out of the boards—and the lefse Bernice was making on the spot. Seventy-five boards had sold out the first day at the Norsk Høstfest in Minot, North Dakota. But could they take your order? (I bought a board and cover, and they work well.)

So in June 1986, Dennis entered the picture and said the family should make a go of selling lefse and related products. Brother Jack helped with the boards and covers. They set up shops in Spicer, Willmar, and New London. They had four outlets in the Twin Cities, and they mailed lefse all over the Upper Midwest. In the peak months of November and December, Jacobs employed twelve bakers who could do up two thousand lefse a day.

Using *instant* potatoes. That's right. Grandma Legwold turned a bit in her grave when Jacobs told me that, but his lefse tasted good. He used instant potatoes because they saved on labor. Imagine peeling three to four hundred pounds of spuds a day before you even started making dough. Potato-peeling devices do rub off the skins, said Jacobs, but you still need a hydrometer to figure out how much water is in each batch of potatoes. Not all potatoes are created equal in water content, and if you don't make adjustments in the recipe according to moisture, you could end up with sticky dough and tough lefse, said Jacobs. Instant potatoes always have the same moisture content; thus, no dinging with the recipe.

So from Jacobs I learned I could use instant potatoes. I prefer real ones, purist that I am, but it's nice to know that if I want to save myself some work I can use instant. I also learned to slip a cotton-polyester sock over my corrugated rolling pin to prevent sticking.

The best tip I got from Jacobs before I left for home was this: Don't grill side one too long. Give that first side of the lefse just a light singe (thirty-five to forty-five seconds), then use your lefse stick to flip the round while it still has most of its moisture for side two. If you like big bold brown spots on your lefse, side one will look pale and ugly to you. But don't despair; brown spots will be on side two and your lefse won't have crunchy edges from overcooking side one. Just serve side two up.

Back home, I made lefse and thought about the tips Jacobs had given me. I thought also that nothing warms up a kitchen on a cold, nasty November night quite like making lefse. I often do it on a Sunday night. The weekend's over and there's work tomorrow, which I don't want to think about quite yet. I want something that keeps me in the present or offers warm memories, so I make lefse. Kate, our three year old, is squealing with delight in the tub. Later Ben, our six year old, and my wife Jane are playing *Chutes and Ladders* or *Go Fish* in the family room with the TV on. They all come into the kitchen, roll a warm one, and we talk. Ben and Kate can be real chatterboxes. They leave for stories before bed.

My rolling pin thumps and squeaks as I roll and listen to the radio. When I flip the rounds, a sweet soft slap assures me all's well on the grill. I think of Grandma and wonder if she heard some of these household sounds when she was rolling and flipping her lefse. I wonder if she looks down on me from wherever she is and says, "My, my, it's *Gary* who's making lefse now. Who would have thought?"

My grill is right in front of the counter window. Steam from the lefse condenses on the now-dark window, making a soft dew in a season of hard frosts. Inside, we're cozy. This is peace.

3

Carl Knutson: Did the Lefse Make Him a Little Loony?

CARL KNUTSON'S LEFSE SONG starts with "I am the nut." He means it as a metaphor; that he was an important part of the lefse-making plant he owned for years, Carl's Norwegian-Maid Lefse in Hawley (pop. 1,634), in the Red River Valley, northern Minnesota. But many people who know Carl have probably *heard* the lyrics as, "I am **A** nut," and they say, "Boy, Carl, you sure got *dat* right, don't you know."

Anyway, here are the lyrics to a song Carl sang for me in his Norwegian-country twang, and years ago to the forty-some lefse makers he employed when he still owned the business. The lyrics reveal a lefse sweatshop this was not. "Mom" was Carl's wife, Lousena, an excellent lefse maker and the heart of the business.

I am the nut.
Mom is the wheel.
Our girls are the spokes
For a perfect deal.
If our girls
Refuse to come,
There'd be no spokes
And the wheel won't run.

"That was something I threw together walking to the bathroom and back," added Carl.

Spend a minute with this rangy seventy-eight-year-old and you begin to wonder. He *was* kinda nutty, in a wonderful way, and always good for a wink and a smile and a laugh or two. He said he had seven fiddles and still told the ladies he liked "to fiddle around. I say I'm old enough to know better but young enough to try."

When he went to Sweden, he said he fooled the locals into believing he was Swedish-American by talking such good Swedish. But after he heard one too many Norwegian jokes, he finally had to put down the Swedes with a taste of their own medicine. He admitted he was Norwegian-American and the reason they all thought he was Swedish was that "he was sick a lot as a kid." The Swedes slapped Carl on the back and they all had a good laugh.

When Lousena died in 1981, it nearly broke Carl. He almost quit the business, if not life, until three of his five children, Pat Gruhl, Gail Dalen, and Steve Knutson, decided to carry on the lefse-making firm Carl and Lousena had started in 1954.

Back then, Carl was a farmer, but more than anything Carl was by nature a salesman. So from fall to New Year's, when farming got slow, he'd sell lefse. Carl started selling lefse using a '47 Chevy. He wore out seven cars on the back-

Carl Knutson: Did the Lefse Make Him a Little Loony?

"At first it was like pulling teeth," said Carl Knutson of the early days of selling lefse out of the back seat of a '47 Chevy. No more, however. His daughter, Pat Gruhl, began in the lefse business when Carl quit. She started Sena's Place, a lefse-making plant in Hitterdal, Minnesota.

roads of Minnesota, North Dakota, and Montana, including an old black '74 Ford LTD with a monstrous 460-cubic-inch motor. This was a ride-in-comfort, lefse-toting machine that would see 300,000-plus miles of the Midwest before it quit. To handle the lefse load, the LTD was equipped with overload springs and six-ply tires. Carl tore out the back seat and wall to the trunk. He'd pack it with ice and a hundred cases of lefse and off he'd go, gone Tuesday through Saturday sometimes.

Carl would work his way through the Red River Valley towns and be in Minot, North Dakota, his first night out.

Then, staying on U.S. 2, it was out to Wolf Point, Montana, or maybe Glasgow, for the second night. If sales were brisk early in the trip, he'd call home and arrange to have a few boxes shipped on a westbound freight train.

For the third night he'd work his way back to Williston, North Dakota, and spend the fourth night at Underwood, just north of Washburn. My maternal grandparents, Emanuel and Elsie Gehring, lived there and farmed a section. On the last day, if he had any lefse left fresh enough to sell, he'd swing down to Bismarck before hightailing it back to Hawley.

Often, sales were not brisk, especially as Carl was just getting going. Skeptical store owners would want a taste of Carl's lefse, and his challenge was to have enough thawed and ready to serve; thawing too much too soon meant spoilage, and thawing too little too late meant too bad when it came to sales.

There were down days when he gave away more than he sold, days of "No thanks" and "Maybe next time." Between rejections, in his motel room or driving on the road to nowhere, Carl had time to dream up songs. He had written nearly forty, he said, including this one about selling lefse and feeling low.

> All those years on the road,
> Lonely hours go by.
> As I sit all alone counting mile after mile,
> My storekeeper says
> I'll be back in a while.
> So I stand there and wait
> with that artificial smile.

"At first it was like pulling teeth," said Carl. On a bright, fabulous February day Carl, with a pretty strong Norwegian accent, was telling me about those early days of pitching lefse. We were sitting in Sena's Place, a lefse-making plant in Hitterdal, Minnesota, (pop. 253) about seven miles north of Hawley.

Pat Gruhl, Carl's daughter who set up Sena's Place in honor of her mother, Lousena, had gone down the street for coffee. There was coffee left by mistake in the pot in the front room, but the coffee was frozen. Sena's had been shut down pretty much since the holidays. The heat was off, and the oval door window was cracked. The sun blazed through the south-facing storefront windows, making the cozy customer area of the plant comfortable, with an open coat and the coffee Pat poured into sturdy, translucent-green china cups. A sign, "Happiness is Homemade", hung on the wall.

As Carl and I chatted, passersby stopped and stared. "They probably think you're from the bank here to foreclose on us," Carl quipped.

Pat was checking her phone-answering machine. She had moved away from home years ago, married, had kids, and moved to the Twin Cities and Iowa. Around the time of Lousena's death she brought her family back home to make a go of it in the lefse business. "Great! Somebody wants our lefse for a wedding, Dad," she said. "Some guy up in Ada. His daughter's getting married and he wants lefse served."

"Well, she wants to be strong for the wedding," said Carl with a chuckle.

Carl wanted to get on with his account of how those early days of lefse selling were tough, plain and simple. Carl said his coming to town, of course, meant he was cutting in on the business of local homemakers/lefse makers, a business that at the holidays was good enough to pay for Christmas gifts, and then some.

Carl's lefse put the storekeeper in a tight spot. The

storekeeper needed the lefse. People could (and still can) get downright desperate for lefse around the holidays; they didn't care where the storekeeper got it—just so he got it. But the storekeeper also needed loyal customers. He did not want to be known as the guy who had any part in depriving Mrs. Olson's granddaughter of a new doll for Christmas. So what to do?

"You see, you had all homemakers then, and every town had at least one woman who was the local lefse maker," said Carl. "She'd cover three to five miles, or maybe two towns. Let's say, now, that here's the town she started in"—Carl tapped his left index finger on the tabletop—"and all around here she'd peddle back and forth. So I'd lose maybe three stores there.

"But she'd just do it for the holidays, Thanksgiving and Christmas. Little by little, storekeepers would come around because I'd go from September right on through to New Year's."

Carl persisted even when a competitor began selling machine-made lefse, versus all hand-rolled, like Carl's—at half the price. "You'd have to be out of your mind to try to do this all over again. It amounts to this: If you hang in long enough and tough enough, eventually you will win. But it just about kills you off in the meantime."

I asked Carl and Pat why lefse was so important to Scandinavians, especially Norwegian-Americans.

"It's hanging on to tradition, that's all," said Carl, fighting to get his word in first over Pat.

Pat began patiently. "When people at Thanksgiving and Christmas sit down to their turkey and dressing and cranberries—"

"—and lutefisk," Carl interjected.

"—and lutefisk," Pat conceded. She was used to Carl's but-ting in. "Well, lefse's always been a part of it. It's always been there. And at Christmas, along with your *fattigmann* and *krumkake*, you have lefse and flatbread and all your other Norwegian pastries. It's tradition.

"I mean, I have had several people call me or write to me and explain: 'We have to have lefse at Christmas. I don't know what we'd do without it. *Please*, you have to send us some lefse.'"

"And what do you do?" I asked.

"I send them their lefse. It's as simple as that." Pat chuckled.

"Now the Germans, they never went for lefse," said Carl. "They went for . . . what is it the Germans go for? . . . I know it, too . . . Uh, well, that sour stuff that you make—sauerkraut. I remember the first time I ate that at my wife's folks, I thought, geez, don't they know that stuff is rotten?"

"If they are Norwegian or have Scandinavian ancestors, they had lefse as children," said Pat. "A lot of these people that we ship lefse to are in Mesa, Arizona, or in Phoenix, or in your Sun Cities—retired Norwegians down there. They are used to having lefse at Christmastime."

Pat paused to light a cigarette, then continued. "As the years have gone by, there isn't anybody who has learned how to make lefse. All the older women knew how to do it—"

Carl jumped in: "And the younger women wanted to do it and couldn't, see—"

"Either that," said Pat, "or just decided they didn't want to do it."

"No, because there was too much mess with it, and they'd just as soon buy it. I've heard that a lot, too," said Carl.

"And, therefore, a lot of the younger generation simply have never gotten into lefse making," said Pat. "Let's say you got a middle-aged housewife, forty-five years old: 'Well my Mom used to make this stuff. I never learned how to do it. Now I have a family, and I want to have this great Christmas dinner. I want lefse. I don't know how to make lefse, and I don't want that machine-made stuff. It's not as good as the homemade; I want the good stuff.' "

"That was my problem to start with," said Carl. "People would ask, 'Is this homemade or machine made?'

"And I said: 'It's homemade.'

"They'd say, 'You can't tell *me* it's homemade. There ain't no way. I roll a lot of lefse, but yours is absolutely like it's printed.'

"Well I said, 'Then come down to the shop and watch the women do it.'

" 'It is actually homemade, then?'

" 'Sure, it's homemade.' "

Pat explained that some lefse-making places cut the edges of the rounds so that they are perfectly round. Here at Sena's, rollers didn't cut edges. "I train a new gal in here to roll lefse, and that first lefse that she rolls out is probably going to be the shape of any lake around here, like Lee Lake, Anderson Lake, whatever. But you learn how to do this."

Carl raised his arm and pointed his finger as he said, "The ladies would come and put their hands on my arm and say, 'How in the world could you make lefse that perfect? You know, I used to hate you.' I took their business away, and I can't blame them. 'But,' they'd say, 'I hate to admit this, but now I'm buying yours.' So, there you got 'er."

A couple older ladies out walking stopped and gave us a blank look that said: "Vat da heck you tink you're doing drinking coffee in a store vith no heat?" Carl smiled at them—he knew them, of course—and said he supposed the town would be buzzing shortly. We topped off our cups.

"I used to have a little old guy come in here all the time," said Pat, "and he was, oh, just a crafty old guy. He was by himself, you know; his wife had passed on, and he'd come in here and visit. He would never admit to me that he liked lefse. He would tease me. He'd come in and buy two packages. He'd say: 'Well, my shoes are getting really bad. I'm going to have to get them resoled. I'm going to have to get them resoled . . ."

"I wonder how many times I heard that," said Carl with a shake of his head. Then Carl leaned back and crowed out a lefse lyric:

> You can use it for a shoe sole.
> You can wear it on the street.
> And some people say that
> It's even fit to eat.

"One guy even had a roll of it in his bathroom," said Carl. Pat shook her head.

I wondered how lefse-making kitchens, which depend so heavily on skilled seasonal labor, could find and keep help. "This will be my eighth year up here," said Pat. "It's gotten harder and harder all the time. Both I and my brother (Steve Knutson, who owned Carl's Norwegian-Maid Lefse) have had a lot of trouble with it because it is a seasonal job.

"The majority of the people I've got working for me are the ones that have stayed with me since I started. They are women, fifty and older, looking for a few bucks at Christmastime. I had a woman work for me the last two years who was sixty-five years old, and she rolled lefse like crazy. She just went to town. But, more and more, it's getting really hard to find good help."

She said her six rollers there at Sena's could put out close to two thousand sheets a day; Carl's, down in Hawley, does six to seven thousand sheets. "We go through," said Pat, "six hundred pounds of potatoes a day. I'm pretty proud of what I've got here. It's not a whole lot but it's mine."

"Did your Mother make good lefse?" I asked Pat. I knew the answer, but I wanted to know more about Lousena.

"Of course, she did everything the best."

"And then she taught you?"

"Mother taught me how to mix the ingredients, and she taught me how to fry lefse, but before she could teach me anything else, she died. And everything else I learned from Dad and on my own. I worked with my Mother only three months before she passed away."

I asked Pat how old she was when her mom died.

"Let's see, she passed away in '81, so I must have been thirty-two."

"So, you just weren't interested in lefse until shortly before she died?"

"No, because I lived away from home for ten years. I moved back in 1980, and at that time Mother and Dad had Carl's lefse. When she passed away, truthfully, Dad wanted to give the business up. My sister, Gail, and I wouldn't let him. We said, 'You've got a good product; you've got a good thing going here. I think you should just keep it going.' "

Carl broke in here: "You got to remember after Mom passed away, I could have just as well gone, too, because I completely depended on her. See, I figured I could dink around until Mom—" He didn't finish the sentence, but nodded his head. Memories.

He went on in a low voice, respectful. "But she was the most wonderful woman. She was like . . . she was a three-way combination. She was like the sister I never had, like a mother—I shouldn't say it—the mother that I never really had, and a wife. You could match that combination, but you could never beat it."

A car pulled up in front of the store. A granddaughter was romping around in the back seat. Grandpa waited in the car. Grandma came in and Carl said *God dag,* "Good afternoon." She said the same and said she wanted lefse. Pat politely said, no, she was closed down for the season.

"Ya, I know," said Grandma. She was short, wearing a scarf. Her name was Myrtle, and from the start she was someone who came right at you. Pat said they should have some over at Ma's Store. Myrtle said Pat's recording on her phone-answering machine said she had some lefse frozen. What about that? Myrtle said she had been in Fargo that morning and was now heading home to Twin Valley. "Dad is bellyachin' " for some lefse, she said, nodding to the car out front.

Pat was perplexed and said she had some at home, in her freezer, but she didn't have any here. Check next door at Ma's Store. The stuff in Pat's freezer would be good enough, said Myrtle. When would Pat be back, then? She started to ask Pat for her phone number, then reconsidered, saying, "It doesn't help me to have your phone number. *You* should have *my* number. When you come here you call me and I'll be here in a little while."

Carl said, *"Hun er ikke saa dum, som du vet,"* "She ain't so dumb, you know."

Pat again asked Myrtle if she was sure that the lefse next door at Ma's Store wouldn't do? "No, I need a whole case," said Myrtle. "When I buy I buy, and I can have lefse all summer, now."

Carl said, *"Det er ikke fattigdom her,"* "There's no poverty here."

Pat said she'd go get the case from her freezer and leave it at Ma's Store. Even that didn't satisfy Myrtle entirely.

"You should bring more than one if you got more," admonished Myrtle, because then Pat could sell to others.

"They're diehards," said Carl to me. He was enjoying this exchange. "They'll drive for that certain product. But it took years to build that."

Pat said she'd get the case to Ma's this afternoon, and Myrtle could leave $27.36 there. Okay? "Ya," said Myrtle, and added for no apparent reason, "I'm Norwegian."

She was heading out and asked if somebody kicked the door window and broke it.

"I was drunk again," said Carl loudly, and with a laugh. "I can say that because I don't drink."

Myrtle didn't miss a beat, and came back with, "Well, I thought probably you did."

Carl laughed at her spunk and said he'd been accused of it many times. Myrtle softened a bit and said to Carl, "And it's real good lefse."

"Oh, I know," said Carl. "If it comes from Carl's it has to be good."

Myrtle opened the door and Pat said "Thank you, Myrtle."

It was getting on toward noon, and I offered to buy lunch. "Well, you don't have to do that," said Pat.

"Oh yeah, he does," said Carl. And he laughed a good one when I said he was not so dumb. Then he translated "not so dumb" into Norwegian for me: *ikke saa dum.*

4

Lazarus Lefse

I WAS SHAKING MY HEAD and staring at this lefse I got
months ago from the good folks at the Sons of Norway
in Story City, Iowa, (pop. 2,762). No way this stuff was
coming back to life. It was dry. It was crusty. It had been sitting on a shelf in my office.

This hard lefse, sometimes called Hardanger or West
Coast lefse, was *supposed* to be like this. It wasn't made with
potatoes —just Crisco or lard dissolved in milk, with sugar,
salt, and flour added later. It was rolled out and grilled, just
like potato lefse, then stacked and stored in a cool dry place.
No refrigeration needed. When you want to eat it, you dip
it in water, let the excess drip off, and soak it between towels
or waxed paper until it's soft and rollable. Add butter and
sugar, and down the hatch.

Had I not seen this lefse being made and then dipped in
water before I ate it, I wouldn't have believed it. I still had
a hard time believing these crispy critters in my office were
going to spring back to life.

I had heard that they made lefse different down in central
Iowa. The Story City folks told me *they* had heard that people made lefse different up there in Minnesota. "So you use
real potatoes in yours, huh? Imagine that. Ya, I've heard of
that."

UFF DA! What the heck is that man doing? Dipping lefse in water!? And why doesn't that woman stop him? Because that's the way they do it at the Sons of Norway in Story City, Iowa. Marian Skartvedt and Merv Tieg made a hard lefse, sometimes called West Coast lefse, in the tradition of many areas of the West Coast of Norway. It can be stored without refrigeration for months.

I had thought all lefse was made with potatoes. Not true. From what I've been able to piece together, there are at least fifty kinds of lefse, some with potatoes, some without. In Norway about a hundred years ago, each region would have its recipe and method of making lefse, which was used almost universally.

I use the word "universally" advisedly because to people in that region, that was their universe. They didn't stray too far from the home place in those days, which meant regional differences in lefse. Story City is just a couple hundred miles across the same state from Decorah, but in terms of lefse making, the two towns are worlds apart.

I walked into the nice new Sons of Norway building in Story City, and the gang was all there. Black crepe hung over a picture of Olav V, the King of Norway who had recently passed away. Merv Tieg put Crisco in a pan of milk, and heated the pan on the stove. As we waited for the Crisco to dissolve, we talked lefse, everyone just kind of leaning on the counters or table and singing out across the big kitchen whatever entered their minds on lefse.

"Well, it's different from McDonald's, lefse is," said Marian Skartvedt.

I asked why that was important.

"Lefse makes us remember what it was like before, in Norway, when times weren't always so good," she said. "Lefse is unique to our roots, and more and more people are interested in their heritage. Lefse's a tradition, a thread running through the family." She showed me a drawing of a 19th century woman who went from house to house in Norway making about a year's supply of lefse for anyone who hired her.

Muriel Melling said in 1880 her great grandparents came over from Enebakk, Norway, north of Olso. They had to travel light on the boat, of course, but one of the items they brought with them was a wide wooden canister in which they stored their lefse during the trip.

By now the Crisco was melted and the dough was ready to roll. The men gathered there that day—Merv, Ray Skartvedt, and Marval Melling—did the rolling while Marian, Alice Miller, and Muriel baked. I said that it was nice to see the men in the kitchen. Alice went over to squeeze Marval's biceps and said the men were strong and could really roll. Marval added, "Ya, with a good strong back and a weak mind, you'll do anything."

Alice had the most beautiful lefse pin I had ever seen. Made of walnut in Norway about a hundred years ago, it was dark and strong. The white flour in the grooves made the grain in the walnut come to life. A deep gnarly flour-filled groove twined around one end of the pin out into the fixed smoothed handle. At first this looked like a serious flaw in the wood, a wound. But as my fingers explored the groove, I wondered if lightning had struck that handle years ago and some of the charge had remained.

Alice rolled rhythmically with her pin, and said while making lefse she often remembered her parents and the huge Christmas Eve family gatherings. She thought of her mother making lefse and storing it in wooden boxes near the entry. I imagined a huge box, a bin, full of dried, dormant lefse waiting for a little moisture so it could spring to life on the night before Christmas.

"Think of the time and effort it took to fill that box," I said aloud.

Marian lamented the fact that nowadays, in an instant-food world, that box would never get filled. "People want that tradition, they want that real taste, but they want somebody else to do it," she said.

Back at my office, months after watching the Story City crew make their hard lefse, I reached up and slid a lefse from the stack they gave me to take home. The lefse was thin and wavy and felt like a newspaper that had been soaked in the rain then dried for weeks in the sun. I shook my head, a doubting Thomas.

I carried this poor dead lefse down to the kitchen, and my wife, Jane, asked what on earth had happened to that lefse. Months before when I returned from Story City, I had told her about how people down there make this hard lefse that

*Alice Miller held the most beautiful lefse rolling pin I'd ever seen.
It was made in Norway about a hundred years ago, and the
white flour in the grooves made the dark walnut come to life.*

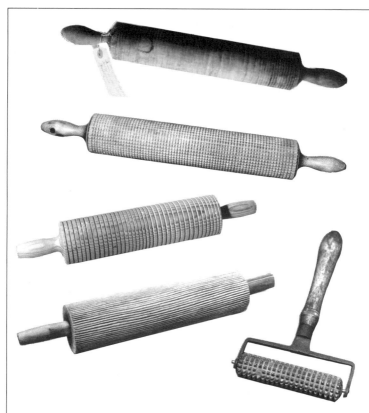

Lefse rolling pins have teeth or grooves that crush lumps and prevent tearing. Grooves also permit even heat distribution. Pins with lengthwise grooves (lower left) are rare but cute. The bone pin with one handle was used more commonly in Norway after the lefse was on the stove. My favorite pin is the top one, which came over from Norway and is more than 160 years old. Now, that family ate a lot of lefse. (Photos by Vesterheim, The Norwegian-American Museum in Decorah, Iowa.)

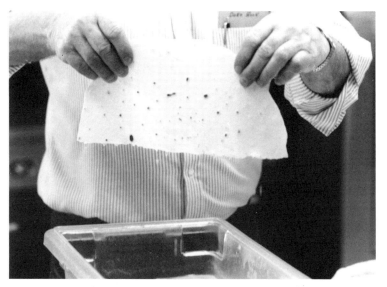

What a sight—water dripping off lefse. To soften this hard lefse, you need to dip it in water about a half hour before eating and then cover it with towels or waxed paper.

needed to be dipped in water before eating, but I don't think she really comprehended it then. And I don't think she thought she'd live to see the day lefse was dipped in water—not in *our* house. She shook her head and returned to reading the paper.

I carefully carried the lefse around the counter to the sink. I didn't want to drop it because it would have shattered and scattered all over the ceramic tile floor. I put about a half inch of water in the sink and, with a here-it-goes shrug, I lowered the lefse and splashed some water on it to revive it. Then I held it up and let the water drain off. I wrapped it in a towel and left it.

I returned in fifteen or twenty minutes to find the wrapped lefse beneath two Twin Cities phone books. Jane had put the phone books there, perhaps subconsciously thinking what harm could two big books do to a dead lefse, anyway.

I lifted off the phone books, and slowly unfolded the towel, expecting to find bits of brittle lefse. But behold, the lefse *had* come back to life! I buttered it and sprinkled sugar on it. Good. I missed the potato taste, but it was amazingly good lefse.

As I chewed my lefse, I ruminated that this, O ye lefse makers of little faith, was the kind of lefse to be served every year at Easter.

5
The Boys of Starbuck and The World's Largest Lefse

W E GATHERED AT GORDY'S CAFE, right there at the corner of Highways 28 and 29 as you came into town. Gordy's was part of the Amoco station there in Starbuck, Minnesota (pop. 1,224). I was there to, well, to just be in the presence of The Boys of Starbuck, who on Saturday, July 1, 1983, barged right into the lore of lefse—in a big way. No, in the biggest way. These nine men of humble origins (the two Swedes had somewhat humbler origins than the rest, said the Norskie Boys) made The World's Largest Lefse.

Maurice Walline was sitting there waiting for me. He was the retired town postmaster who also used to own a hardware store. A sharp, active guy who loved to laugh. At the hint of humor, his eyes watered, he colored to the top of his bald head, and a tide of forced air gushed out from him, almost as if he'd been socked in the solar plexus.

On July 1, 1983, The Boys of Starbuck rolled into the lore of lefse by making The World's Largest Lefse.

(Photos courtesy of Ron Lindquist and The Starbuck Times.*)*

Maurice explained to me he was a Swede in a Norwegian town. He gushed as I told him what Ann Lindquist, Assistant Publisher and Bookkeeper of *The Starbuck Times*, told me about Swedes in Starbuck. When her Swedish husband, Ron Lindquist, the weekly's publisher and editor, came to town, the elders told him they only let ten Swedes in Starbuck—and he was the ninth.

Into Gordy's came Tilford Jergenson. Big guy, pure Norwegian. His brother Luverne Jergenson would arrive later. Then came Maurice Amundson, thoughtful and polite, wearing a ski sweater. He was followed by Chuck Wahlquist, the other Swede, a lawyer looking dapper in his suit and tie. John Gorder, a carpenter, came in last, sitting and pushing his cap back on his head. Larry Kittelson, a baker who owned the Pastry Shop Bakery over in Glenwood and Roller of The World's Largest Lefse, couldn't make it that day. Earl Larson also couldn't make it, and Julius Aaberg, who had made the grill by welding together two $5 \times 10'$ ¼-inch steel sheets, had passed away. These, then, were The Boys of Starbuck.

Walline held up the *Schibsted Norwegian Book of Records* that had a picture of The Boys of Starbuck making their masterpiece. "You'll notice, in the foreground, here is a Swede and here is a Swede, right in this Norwegian book of records," Walline said, beaming.

"I don't think that went over too good in Norway," said Tilford, and Walline gushed.

Tilford showed Amundson a postcard of The Boys of Starbuck setting the record. Tilford said that the Swedes had been blocked out in the picture by the Norskie Boys. Amundson said, "That's a good photographer." More gushing and laughter.

But now it was time to get down to the business of telling

how The Boys of Starbuck—The So-Fine Nine, The Lords of Lefse—grabbed a piece of history.

Starbuck was planning Heritage Days around its centennial, and members of the Lions Club wanted all lefse-loving eyes, for one brief shining moment, to look to this small town on the shores of Lake Minnewaska. The plan was to make The World's Largest Lefse.

The week before the July 1st Centennial Celebration The Boys of Starbuck scheduled a couple of practice runs, on Monday and Thursday; anyone knows you didn't just roll out of bed on Saturday morning and roll out The World's Largest Lefse, just like that, don't ya know.

Aaberg's 10 × 10′ steel grill was lugged down to the train depot and centered over the tracks. Charcoal—some six hundred pounds of it, supplied by Kingsford, for the two practice runs and the big day itself—was spread and lit under the grill. I asked if trains were still running on those tracks at the time. Amundson, the Dean of Dry Humor, said no, "but if there had been, there would have been plenty of time between trains. Anyhow, they probably would have stopped for lefse."

The dough for each run was made up of thirty pounds of instant potatoes, supplied by Pillsbury, thirty-five pounds of flour (give or take a pound or two, depending on the wind), one pound of sugar, one pound of powdered milk, and four pounds of shortening. Land o' Lakes supplied all the butter.

The two practice runs were miserable flops because it was hot that week and The Boys couldn't get that big glob of dough cooled down well enough. It rolled okay, but fell apart into chamois-like sheets when they transferred it to the grill. Kittelson, the baker, tinkered with the recipe, desperately trying to find the right combination of ingredients to toughen up the lefse a tad.

"We had a community from down south, Clarkfield, Minnesota, that was at one of our practice runs," recalled Wahlquist. "They were taking notes on what was going on and wanted to make one bigger than ours for their centennial. After they saw us do it, well, we haven't heard from them since."

Wahlquist paused and then looked at me in suspiciously before asking with a straight face, "Are you sure you're not from Clarkfield?"

It's safe to say that The Boys of Starbuck slept fitfully — if at all — the night before the big day. Word had spread across the land that they were going for the record, albeit with a pretty spotty track record. You talk about pressure, whew! A thousand people had gathered at the depot, not a few of them doubters that *this* crew could pull it off. Cameras were everywhere. A TV crew from Alexandria was coming, the Wilmar paper was there, and WCCO radio in Minneapolis plugged the event. Indeed, for The Boys, this was gut-check time.

The dough had been mixed and cooled real good, and now when the heat was on — it was a real July cooker that day — "Ever-Cool" Kittelson, the baker, took charge with the first critical part in making The World's Largest Lefse: the rolling. A bedsheet was spread on three $4 \times 8'$ sheets of plywood that were centered on an $8 \times 16'$ hay rack Gorder wheeled in special for the occasion. A five-gallon bucket of flour was within arm's reach on the hay rack.

Kittelson decided, wisely, that this was not the time to roll a fancy thin delicacy. "Be Safe, Be Thick" was his thinking. They had plenty of dough, and there was no use leaving any of it in the walk-in cooler a block away, not with the record on the line. Plus, Kittelson, who had gone back to the drawing board with his dough recipe, had come up with

Larry Kittelson sized up his task of turning this big glob of dough into The World's Largest Lefse. Whew, the pressure.

a new shortening: something called puff paste shortening used by bakers to make apple turnovers. This stuff has a high melting point and is sort of the Elmer's Glue of shortenings. Kittelson said he went with puff paste shortening "because we had to have something that was going to hold this big lefse together."

So using three-foot rolling pins (actually, rollers taken from an old grain binder) covered with cloth, Kittelson rolled it about as thick as a shingle—"well reinforced," said Amundson—and hoped it was thick enough to hold together as they got it on the roller and then onto the grill.

Speaking of the grill, I asked, how did you know it would be hot enough to properly cook the lefse? Tilford looked me in the eye and said, "When the grill started smoking and got almost red, we figured it was hot enough." The grill got so hot it started to curl at the edges. Clamps were brought in to stop the curling. Gorder was sweating so much that he eventually developed heat sickness.

The second critical part in making The World's Largest Lefse was getting the rolled out product from the hay wagon to the nearby grill, by now sending off a powerful heat from the coals scattered around the railroad tracks. Much has been made of The World's Largest Lefse, but it would not have been possible without what was surely The World's Largest Rolling Pin. This was a piece of work that was created by Walline, the Swede. It was used only during that fateful week. Now it rested in peace in the depot, which had been converted into a museum.

The roller was made by slipping a twelve-foot metal pipe (one inch) through six one-foot plywood circles with holes drilled in the centers. The circles were spread evenly on the pipe, and pine strips, ⅜-inch wide, were nailed to the circles to fill out the roller.

"The thing about it is, with the one-foot diameter circles—actually it was a little bit more than one foot—we could make three turns with that roller and have the nine feet of lefse on there, because of the circumference of that circle," said Walline. Say what? I asked, confused. Walline explained that $C = 2 \text{ pi} \times r$, or circumference equals 2 $(3.14) \times .5$ feet. Thus the circumference of The World's Largest Rolling Pin approximated 3.14 feet. Three turns with the roller would be enough to pick up a nine-foot lefse.

Why a diameter of nine feet, I asked. What had been the previous record? There was a pause, and truth be told no one

A six-deep crush of about a thousand people had to be cordoned off as The Boys rolled out The World's Largest Lefse on a hay rack wheeled in special for Starbuck's centennial celebration. Here The Boys began to drape this lefse "rug" over what was undoubtedly The World's Largest Roller—twelve feet long— which was needed to carry the lefse to the nearby grill.

really knew what the pre-existing record was, or even if there was such a thing. But if there was, nine feet surely would top it. And they could have gone bigger, said Wahlquist, but they ran out of grill space.

The big roller, it turned out, was really a carrier, not a roller. The Boys had experimented with turning the lefse with "shovels," as Wahlquist described them. Actually, they were pieces of tin attached by Gorder to broom handles. They didn't work too hot, so Walline came up with using a big roller for transporting and turning.

It was time for the lefse "rug" to be draped over the roller and carried to the grill by five men, one on each end of the roller and three holding the lefse in place. Talk about drama. They spread the lefse on the grill and took stock, scratching their heads and pondering just what they had created.

And now for the moment. Gorder, the carpenter, and Wahlquist pulled a tape measure across the widest parts of the lefse: nine feet eight inches by nine feet one inch! The Boys had done it. They had made The World's Largest Lefse.

The Boys carefully turned the lefse over and baked side two. Then it was eating time. "Every bit of it was buttered and passed out—and eaten—except a piece about like this," said Wahlquist, holding his hands a couple feet apart, "which was taken by a pilot and flown down to Governor

The grill, made with two welded 5 x 10' ¼-inch steel sheets, was centered over charcoal coals piled around abandoned railroad tracks. Here, a couple of The Boys held shovels custom-made for the job of turning The World's Largest Lefse over so that the second side could be grilled.

And now for the moment. Cameras were poised as The Boys pulled a tape measure across the widest parts of the lefse and announced: "Nine feet eight inches by nine feet one inch!" The Boys had done it. They had made The World's Largest Lefse.

Perpich [who later sent them a congratulatory letter.] Yeah, when we got it buttered and everything, the people just cheered—you wouldn't believe it. It was really something. They knew what was going on. They all wanted a piece of the action," if not the lefse.

Heady with victory, The Boys decided to tee it up again, so to speak, maybe break their own record. "We made two that day," said Gorder, "and the second one fell apart on us. But that dough he [Kittelson] had made the same day, and it hadn't been chilled as long."

So at that point, having gone one-for-four for the week— but their one was The Big One—The Boys decided to take their record and run. They went up to Star Lanes, the eight-lane bowling ally, for a few well-earned beers.

*All evidence of The World's Largest Lefse was eaten up
immediately by the ecstatic witnesses of lefse-making history.
A piece of the record round was flown to Governor Perpich,
who later sent them a congratulatory note.*

It was time for the boys and me at Gordy's to pay up for
the coffee and go, but not before one parting shot at the
Swedes. We were talking about why lefse was so popular.
"After you eat lutefisk, anything is going to taste good," said
Amundson. He then said that Sweden didn't have lefse, and
Tilford, who had been to Norway and Sweden, offered an
explanation that smacked of social Darwinism, with the
Norwegians winding up in a higher order. "No, Sweden, you
know, they hadn't gotten as far along as the Norwegians at
the time lefse came about."

"Boy, oh boy," said Wahlquist, amid the gusts of laughter. "You were waiting to get that one in."

A smiling Tilford explained to me, "This goes on every day." Then he picked up the postcard of The World's Largest Lefse and said, "There's been a lot laughs over that lefse."

I found this poem/recipe in the *Centennial Cook Book* by the Lutheran Church Women in Starbuck.

> Yew tak yust ten big potatoes
> Den yew boil dem till dar done.
> Yew add to dis some sveet cream
> And by cups it measures vun.
> Den yew steal tree ounces of butter
> An vit two fingers pinch some salt.
> Yew beat dis wery lightly
> If it ain't gude it iss your fault.
> Den yew roll dis tin vit flour
> An light brown on stove yew bake.
> Now call in all Scandihuvians
> Tew try da fine lefse yew make.

6
Lefse, a Pabst, and a Chip Shot

I N THE WORLD of lefse making, John Glesne was a man among women.

Go into any community and ask who are the good lefse makers, and invariably the names you hear are female. That's not surprising, but for a male lefse maker like myself, it is a bit disappointing.

Sure, I know in the old days men brought home the bacon and women fried it up in a pan, but still, these are the '90s. In my search for lefse makers, my thinking was there must be some human being walking this earth who could make a decent round of lefse in spite of, or maybe because of, the Y chromosome he carried. Lefse making is not a sex-linked characteristic. That is, what's in the lefse is separate from what's in the genes. Right?

I asked this of Dr. Marion Nelson, director of Vesterheim, the Norwegian-American Museum in Decorah, Iowa (pop. 8,063). I said that I was looking for a man who made lefse, Steps A through Z, not another male who had been trained to dutifully sit by the grill or stove and flip a round when the lefse master barked, "Flip!"

John Glesne. In the world of lefse making, he was a man among women. Roll on, John.

Oh sure, said Nelson, men *could* make lefse. In fact, he said, we've got one here in town. Call John Glesne.

I did and we met at his home one February evening. He was really going to make lefse? I got to see this, I told myself. I met his wife, Ann, and we all chatted a bit about lefse. About how John had been making lefse for twenty years, about how that was all he made, lefse and pies. About how he "learned by do" mostly, but also by remembering how his mother, Josephine Glesne, used to make it on an old wood stove that was too hot one minute and too cool the next. "I figured if my mother made lefse, then, by golly, I could," said John.

John had the dough prepared when I arrived, and he started rolling. I looked for telltale signs of an imposter, such as the what-do-I-do-here-next kind of pauses. When Ann returned to the den next to the kitchen to continue watching TV, I waited for sideways glances from John to Ann, who could coach through the hallway if she wanted to, without being seen by me.

But no, John was smooth and confident. He kneaded flour into his dough with vigor, and did not fret about adding too much or too little flour, as beginners do. He rolled and turned in a loosey-goosey-at-the-elbows kind of way. No tension or performance anxiety here. His lefse were big and round—and tasty. Ah, here was a man who could make lefse, and then give me a tip or two on turning with one stick.

Glesne's skills—in combination with his gender—had been scrutinized before. Turns out he made lefse during Nordic Fest, Decorah's annual celebration of Nordic heritage in late July. John rotated with other lefse makers, rolling behind a storefront window for the benefit and amusement of passersby, who knew a lefse maker when they saw one and who often did a double-take when they saw the sixty-three-year-old Glesne at the grill. "They just look at me kinda strange," he said with a shrug and wry smile.

If being point man at Nordic Fest for male lefse makers bothered him, he didn't show it. It probably didn't matter much to him. However, one year at Nordic Fest the heat got to Glesne—and to his dough. He had the twelve-to-two shift that day, making lefse in the "fishbowl." Hot day. His dough was a "soggy mess" because of it, he recalled. The parade had just ended and among the throngs watching Glense's every move were a few older ladies front and center, studying, analyzing, poised to pounce on any mistake this man made.

Glesne remembered sweat dripping off the end of his nose onto the lefse as he rolled. Did they notice, the ladies in front? "I'd roll two rounds and they'd be okay," said Glesne with a laugh, "but then that third one would stick and tear. The ladies just stood in front and shook their heads."

Glesne then asked, "Hey, wanna beer?" Sure, I said. I had never had beer with lefse. He pulled out a Pabst Light and rolled out the last few rounds in the batch. We talked some about the Persian Gulf War, and a bit about the insurance business he was in. It was getting near time to go, and he wrapped a few rounds in aluminum foil for me. To get to the front door I needed to go through the front room, where a pitching wedge and a few golf balls were scattered about. A short bucket was placed next to the couch, across the room from the balls and club.

"What's this?" I asked.

Immediately, a sheepish grin took over his face as he bent over to pick up the club. This—golf, that is—was Glesne's passion, he said, as he rested his hands on the club head and crossed his legs, the classic waiting-to-putt stance. Ann re-joined us and she nodded in agreement. He admitted he got out three to four times a week in season and boasted that he had played the local course, Silvercrest, in each month of the year. Of course, in December you had to have some cooperation from the weather, he said.

"What's the bucket for?" I asked.

Well, during TV commercial breaks, he would stroll out to the carpeted front room for a little pitching practice. I was about to ask for a demonstration, but I didn't have to. John was already crouched a step away from a golf ball, taking a practice swing. The house was silent, except for the TV noise in the den. John was in "the zone." He looked at his target one last time. I almost expected him to step back and size up his shot again. But, no, he wiggled a bit and drew the club head back. Again, no performance anxiety here; no hesitation or heebie-jeebies. The club head swept under the ball, which arched toward the couch. Bingo! A bank shot off the base of the couch and into the bucket.

"Look at that!" he said, beaming.

I congratulated him. Then I thanked the both of them and left. I started up my van, grinning and shaking my head about the "The Shot." I drove away thinking lefse he likes, but golf he loves.

7
Lefse, Potatoes, and Occupied Norway

BITTEN NORVOLL and I came up from making lefse in the basement of her south Minneapolis home. She made lefse on top of her washer and dryer and had lefse in her home all year round. In the living room her husband, Torbjorn, in the chair reading the paper, asked if I was Norwegian. I said half; the other half's German. He gave a hint of a smile and said to me: *Du er nodvendigvis ikke en darlig mann forde om du er Norske.* "Just because you're Norwegian doesn't mean you're a bad guy."

Bitten and Torbjorn came to Minnesota in 1950 from Norway, where they were born and raised. Both were from towns north of the Arctic Circle; Bitten was from Narvik, a seaport on Ofotfjorden, the Ofot Fjord, and Torbjorn was from Andenes, on Andøya, a northern island in the Vesteralen chain.

In Norway women would travel from house to house spending
three or four days making up to a year's supply of lefse for the
household. They would often work over an open fire and by
lantern light into the evening. This drawing shows such a woman
rolling in front of an oven. The finished rounds were stacked in
barrels. Rounds were also stored in kistes (sea chests) or steamer
trunks for fishermen packing provisions for long sea voyages.
Often, the shed where this baking took place was also where beer
was made. (The drawing was provided by Marian Skartvedt of
Ellsworth, Iowa. It was a gift from Jon Lairfall, a writer and
artist Marian visited at his home near Trondheim, Norway.)

Vesteralen is just north of the great fishing islands, the Lofotens, on which are located cod fisheries. In years gone by especially, lefse was important to the men who would leave their villages and hire on as fishermen, January through March. In preparation for the fishing season, women of the villages would spend days, in a festive atmosphere, baking lefse and flatbread for the men. Bakers, sometimes working over an open fire, would often work by lantern light late into the evening. In some areas, individual women would go from home to home, spending three to four days making lefse and flatbread for the fisherman of the house. The lefse and flatbread were stacked in barrels, *kistes* (sea chests), or steamer trunks, which were lugged on board. "Each man provided his own food on the boat," said Torbjorn.

Weather made the work dangerous at times, said Torbjorn; "some fishermen paid with their lives." But fishing was good, and the men shipped home crates of fish. Much of their catch, however, they sold to fisheries. Sometimes the men stayed in bunkhouses owned by fisheries. There the men prepared "festive meals" on Sunday afternoons, which included cod and lefse, said Torbjorn. Or they relaxed with their coffee and lefse. "Lefse was a big part of their provisions," he said.

Torbjorn was a bookkeeper in Norway, and Bitten worked as a cook and waitress. Shortly before they migrated, they married and moved to Oslo, where it was hard to find work, said Bitten. They soon decided to give it a go in America, and traveled to Fosston, Minnesota, (pop. 1,599) where Torbjorn had an uncle who was a baker. Bitten went to work at his bakery and Torbjorn, not trusting his English was good enough yet for bookkeeping work, hired on as a house painter.

A handsome Torbjorn and Bitten Norvoll three months after coming to America. On the front lawn of their apartment in Fosston, Minnesota, Bitten held Torbjorn's cousin, Dan Dahl. Lack of work forced the Norvolls, who contemplated returning to Norway, to move to Minneapolis. (Norvoll Photo)

"It was hard to leave family back in Norway," said Bitten, who began preparing lunch for Torbjorn and me. "But we were young and adventurous. We'd never move back. Torbjorn wanted to initially, but now we identify more with America." Torbjorn added that today there are more Norwegian-Americans than Norwegians; Norway's population is just over four million.

Their move to America came five years after World War II ended, which, of course, ended the three-year German occupation of Norway. Both Bitten and Torbjorn vividly remembered that occupation, and recalled how lefse and especially the potato helped prevent many Norwegians from going hungry.

By the way, this was not the first time potatoes had saved hungry Norwegians. Doris Barnaal at Vesterheim in Decorah, Iowa, has looked into the important role the potato played in Norwegian history and gave me the following background information, which I have summarized:

The potato, native to the Andes mountains of Peru and Bolivia, was introduced to Europe by the Spanish in the 16th century, and to Norway in the mid-1700s.

At first, some thought potatoes to be poisonous. But by the early 1800s, Norwegians knew what to do with a potato. In fact, potatoes caught on so well that by 1835 potato crops were six times larger than they had been in 1809. Virtually every home had its own potato patch, even the homes above the Arctic Circle. Poor soil and a short growing season didn't affect the highly nutritious potato, and the yield from potatoes was four or five times better than from wheat or rye.

The potato became a family's insurance policy against starvation where grains could not grow because of climate or bad weather. It was eaten as is and was a fine extender in soups, sausages, and daily breads such as lefse.

The acceptance and then dependence on the potato contributed to overpopulation in the 1800s, which eventually contributed to migration to America. From 1800 to 1865, the Norwegian population nearly doubled to more than 1.7 million. The economy was generally good, there was peace, there was the discovery of the smallpox vaccination and improvement in sanitary conditions, and potatoes and protein-rich herring became the staple foods for poor people. Thus, people lived longer and the population boomed, pushing people out of crowded areas to northern Norway, where land was still available and fishing was good, and to America.

Later, during the German occupation of Norway in World War II, the potato again was important, according to Bitten and Torbjorn. In Norway, a potato cake-like lefse called lompe "kept us alive," said Bitten. "We very much lived on potatoes then. I tell you, there was not much food. What food there was, the Germans used for the troops. The Germans would take the fresh fish, and the stores and restaurants would get the rotten fish."

Our talk took place during the Persian Gulf War, and Bitten said she "feels sorry for the Iraqis. I know Hussein is crazy, but he won't suffer; the people will. They won't have food and water." (As it turned out, she was right, according to post-war reports from Iraq.)

"But during the occupation we could buy potatoes," she continued, "and we knew so many ways of using potatoes. We couldn't buy much milk or butter or margarine—or a decent flour. The flour we could buy was so heavy. You'd bake bread, and the outside was hard and crusty and the inside just a lump of dough."

By now, Bitten had put the finishing touches on a fabulous lunch including open-faced sandwiches of crab and shrimp, *gjetost* (goat cheese), and three kinds of lefse. She said over her shoulder that during the occupation Norwegians were forced to turn out lights at night and read only German newspapers. Radios were not allowed, but people in the remote North were known to break the ban. If caught with a radio, you were jailed, said Bitten. Germans found out about a radio owned by her uncle in the northern mountains, but he fled to Sweden, evading German troops.

Torbjorn said the Germans weren't about to occupy every town; Norway is a big country. He said if you kept the southern tip of Norway where it is and then swung the northern tip south as far as it would go, it would reach into northern Africa. Nevertheless, the Germans did occupy key cities exceedingly well. Narvik's port was ice-free year-round. It is not far from Sweden's border, and the Swedes used the port extensively to ship iron ore, said Bitten. In fact thirty-five percent of the population of Narvik was Swedish. The Germans seized this key seaport, but not without a fight. Bitten said Narvik was one of the last sites of fighting resistance to the occupation.

Andenes, Torbjorn's home town, was a strategic military site for the Germans. Torbjorn remembered December 1942, when German troops began rolling into town.

Why didn't they fight? Torbjorn said he'd been asked that several times since the war. "I tell people they would have done the same thing we did. There were sixty-five hundred troops that entered a town with a population of eighteen hundred and fifty. We knew they were there," he said in a grim understatement.

"Two days before Christmas my family was told we had twenty-four hours to get out of the house, or we'd be thrown out bodily."

Torbjorn said the Germans took over the finer houses in town, converting them to barracks and such. His family moved to an apartment above a store; three rooms for traveling officers were also on the floor. His family's house, which his family didn't re-occupy until three months after the war ended, was converted to a hospital.

Torbjorn said the family could still use the basement of

their house-turned-hospital for things like storing vegetables. He went back to the house for the first time and noticed the floor had been gouged by the hobnail boots worn by the soldiers. He entered the living room, where there was a black marble hearth. There, a soldier was splitting wood right on the marble hearth. Torbjorn stopped and stared, incredulous.

"The soldier stopped and saw me staring at him," said Torbjorn. "He said, 'What are you looking at?'

"I said, 'You. Do you do that in your own living room?'

"He got all red in the face and finally said, 'I'm awful sorry, but I've been a soldier for three years now.' Most of the soldiers were decent fellows. You had the most trouble with the young ones who were indoctrinated."

We began to eat and I asked the Norvolls why lefse was so important to Norwegian-Americans. Torbjorn said that with emigrants in the early part of this century especially, "whenever they left, it was goodbye forever. So they would cling to anything—old diets, memories—anything that reminded them of the old country."

Bitten added that for years you couldn't buy lefse in stores, so to have lefse you had to make it yourself. Going through the motions of making lefse evokes far more memories, she said, than simply plunking down the cash in a store for a lefse package.

Speaking of lefse, it was time to taste each of the three kinds Bitten had prepared. Torbjorn got up to get the mail. He returned saying, with his dry humor, "The mailman has been here, or it might have been a female mailman." Bitten, meanwhile, explained the differences between the lefse she had prepared. For seventeen years she taught a cooking class at the Minneapolis Technical Institute. She was retired now.

So you don't make lefse because it's so messy, huh. Try making it in your basement, as Bitten Norvoll did in her home in Minneapolis. Bitten, who with her husband Torbjorn came over from her native Norway in 1950, had vivid memories of how potatoes and lefse prevented many from going hungry in occupied Norway in World War II.

The potato lefse, of course, I knew about. She said that in Norway most of the fifty or so kinds of lefse were not made with potatoes. However, the lompe was a popular potato pancake used to wrap hot dogs in. And potato lefse was made, especially inland, in the Osterdal valley.

Bitten's other two kinds of lefse were not made with potatoes. *Krinalefse* was made with eggs, sugar, buttermilk or sour cream, butter, whipping cream, soda, and lemon rind. Flour was added to the dough, which was rolled and grilled just like potato lefse. *Krinalefse*, which could be kept in an airtight container in a cool place for weeks, was found most in northern Norway. A mix of butter, sugar, whipping cream, and cardamom is spread between two pieces of *krinalefse*, which was cut in a distinctive diamond shape.

Mør (which means tender) lefse was cut in a triangle shape. The dough was made of sour cream, sugar, white corn syrup, butter, eggs, hartshorn powder, and water. Flour was used to roll it out, then it was baked in an oven only on one side. A filling of butter, sugar, whipping cream, and cinnamon went between the triangles. *Mør* lefse was popular all over Norway, said Bitten, but especially in the West and North.

All three kinds of lefse were popular all over my tummy that day. Hey, I'm partial to potato lefse, but the other two slid down real slick. After I had my fill, I asked if, like Bitten herself, Norwegians always keep lefse on hand in their homes. Not usually, she said. In fact a few years back she worked at Camp Norway, in Sandane on Nordfjord, on Norway's west coast. There she made lefse and flatbread. The way the happy campers reacted, you would have thought lefse and flatbread had been banned for the summer by proclamation of the king. "They said, 'Oh, this is so good,' " said Bitten. " 'And somebody had to come from the United States to make it.' "

8

Excuse Me,
But Lefse Is Not
a Napkin

Y OU CAN ALWAYS TELL the strangers at our church's
annual fall lutefisk supper," said Eunice Stoen. "They
always unfold the lefse and put it on their laps as
napkins."

Euny's church—everyone called Eunice "Euny"—was the
Big Canoe Lutheran Church, a big brick hilltop country
church thirteen miles northeast of Decorah, Iowa (pop.
8,063). Euny's father, William T. Hexom, was pastor there
for twenty-five years, until he died in 1965.

From my seat at the dinner table in Euny's farmhouse, I
could see Big Canoe and its adjoining graveyard, where Wilbur Stoen's people had been buried. Wilbur, Euny's husband, and son, Bill Stoen, farmed this two-Harvestore, 604-
acre dairy/hog operation. Wilbur's family had been farming
in these parts since 1850, when they first came over from
Norway.

Eunice Stoen, who once made lefse for a New York City party thrown by actress Arlene Dahl, said many native Norwegians touring the United States are drawn to Decorah, Iowa. "They look around and say, 'You're more Norwegian here than we are,' " she said.

Wilbur, a handsome broad-shouldered, square-jaw guy, marched into the house right before lunch (some lunch: ham, brussels sprouts, rolls, an apple/raisin salad, coffee), gave me a once-over, and asked what part of Norway my people came from. No one had ever asked me that before. I said I didn't know and realized I was more than a little puzzled how this basic piece of family history had escaped me.

Well, we may be related, he said, and went to get one of his thick family-tree books. With a big sausage-like finger he pointed to all the Leikvolds in his family tree. Part of Wilbur's family came over from Hallingdal, Norway, and another part from Voss. Part of Euny's family came from the Toten area, north of Oslo. I admitted I vaguely remembered something about my name, Legwold, once being Leikvold. But who had changed it, and when, I had no idea, I said.

The year before, Wilbur had had open heart by-pass surgery. He was fine, now, he said. Euny pointed out that there was no salt on her table, and Wilbur was making an effort to walk regularly. "I try to," he said with a smile, but whenever he went out walking the roads, it wasn't but a few minutes, usually, and a neighbor would recognize him, pull the pickup over, roll down the window, and ask if Wilbur was having trouble or if he needed a lift. I kidded Wilbur that to get in his undisturbed walk, he was going to have to start sneaking out at night wearing a wig or something.

Euny passed the ham for a second time, and I asked who taught her to make lefse. She said Ida Sacquitne, maybe thirty years ago. Ah yes, Ida the Great. I had heard of her, I said. Like all lefse makers, Euny had paid her dues with a bad batch or two in those early days. She said sometimes all she could do was roll out puny eight-inch "rounds" that looked more like a "map of the state of Texas" than anything else. Luckily, Wilbur would be waiting in the wings, saying, sure, he'd take care of her mistakes for her. No problem. Euny said she once tried rolling lefse on Tupperware, "which was for the birds—and so was the lefse."

But she got the hang of it, and was considered in the same league with the best lefse makers, including Ida the Great. Euny, of course, had organized lefse making for the Big Canoe lutefisk-lefse dinner in late October/early November. "You oughta come down for it," she said to me. "We make about forty-five dozen lefse in a day, which serves about five hundred people. Yeah, we get twenty-five to thirty people together at the church to make lefse. We got eight grills going and coffee pots and all. Keep blowing fuses. We've had to rewire the church twice."

In addition to rolling lefse for the flock, Euny had also rolled lefse for the stars. On November 28, 1987, King Olav V of Norway brushed aside his protesting advisers, who warned him not to drive on icy roads to Decorah, where Vesterheim was having a luncheon recognizing fellows and the honorary committee of Vesterheim's national campaign. The king came in the wake of sanding trucks, said Euny, but he made it. He joined actresses Arlene Dahl and Celeste Holm for the festivities, which included a meal with lefse on the menu.

Dahl returned to New York, where she was planning a Christmas dinner party. She wanted lefse on her menu and called Vesterheim director, Dr. Marion Nelson, for the name of a lefse maker. Try Eunice Stoen, said Nelson. Dahl did, and Euny mailed out about a dozen lefse for the party. Shortly after Christmas, Euny received a note from Dahl: The lefse had been the "hit of the party."

It's not unusual for native Norwegians, albeit a wee bit less notable than the king of Norway, to visit Decorah as they tour the United States. "They look around and say,

'You're more Norwegian here than we are,' " said Euny.

"What do they mean?" I asked.

Euny said Norway, like any modern country, changes and evolves. Old ways die off, travel and communications improve, dialects become less distinct, and what is native Norwegian may be taken for granted at times. The question among Norwegians secure in their homeland and heritage is: "What's new and exciting in the world?"

However, among Norwegian-Americans, especially the early immigrants dazed by the exciting new day in a raucous melting pot of a country and feeling increasingly adrift and distanced from their homeland and heritage, the question was, and is: "What's old and established?" "New" swirled all around them, which was fine as long as they centered themselves with the old ways and the things they remembered about the loved ones they left behind, with mixed emotions.

So because Norwegian-Americans had left their evolving homeland and then clung so lovingly and desperately to these old ways, time stopped. That is, the way things were when they left Norway had been, in many cases, "put under glass," so to speak, and revered in Norwegian-American communities such as Decorah.

Euny said Norwegian scholars occasionally travel to Decorah and other communities in Iowa and Minnesota and talk with the old-timers, just to hear the old Norwegian dialects and see the old ways of life that have been passed down and preserved.

Several people, including Euny and Wilbur, told me that, in traveling to Norway or in speaking with Norwegians visiting America, they were surprised to find how ho-hum, if not disdainful, many Norwegians were about lefse and lutefisk. Norwegians eat lutefisk and certainly make lefse in a variety of ways. But many Norwegians couldn't understand why

Potato grinders preceded ricers. Spuds were put in the hole, squished, and augered out. (Photos by Vesterheim, The Norwegian-American Museum in Decorah, Iowa.)

Norwegian-Americans were so enthralled with what they considered to be peasant food.

It is puzzling, and the best explanation I've heard is this: Perhaps it is *because* lefse and lutefisk were once peasant food that kept families alive in bleak times—both in Norway and in America—that today Norwegian-Americans honor lefse and lutefisk so. Besides that, they taste good. Well, lefse anyway.

"Well," announced Euny as she rose to clear the table, "it's time we made some lefse." Wilbur and Bill put their coats on and went back out to work. As she added flour to the dough, I flipped through one of two cookbooks written by Euny (she was working on a third). This one, called *Euny's Cookbook*, had a lefse recipe. At the bottom of the page was a bit of humor. It said, "Fibber McGee's definition of a farm: He said a farm is a hunk of land on which, if you get up early enough mornings and work late enough nights, you'll make a fortune—if you strike oil!"

On the next page she had a lefse kling recipe (lefse with taco-like fixings on top of it). On the bottom of that page was "Apt definition: Brussels sprouts—cabbage after taxes."

I remarked that her lefse recipe used powdered sugar and, for shortening, all butter. She said powdered sugar "makes things fluffy" and butter added color, taste and texture. Then she started to roll.

She said she sold lefse to individuals and stores. I asked if she and other lefse makers she knew had ever been inspected. Inspected? The idea seemed ludicrous. She said, "I worry more about what I eat in some Hardee's or McDonald's than about eating what some Norwegian lady made in her house."

Just then Ned, who had been banging around in the basement fixing the furnace, came to the door to say he was done, the furnace was working fine. Euny offered him some lefse. No, he was in a hurry. After the door closed and he drove off, I said he must have been in a real hurry to turn down warm lefse. Wilbur said with a chuckle, "No, he's German." Wilbur had just "happened" to come back in the house, saying, sure, he'd take care of Euny's mistakes for her. "Tough job, but somebody's got to do it," he said with a big grin.

I asked if I could see his family book again. A few of those Leikvold names seemed vaguely familiar, but I just didn't know. Maybe it was time for me to look into this.

9

Bashed at The Bake Shoppe by The Ladies of Lefse

I HAD BEEN TOLD Spring Grove, Minnesota, (pop. 1,275) was about a hundred and ten percent Norwegian. But when I talked with locals, such as Edna and Palmer Bergsgaard, they said emphatically, "not any more." Still, a big sign—"*Velkommen til Spring Grove*"—was posted on the edge of town on Highway 44, and old timers could be heard jabbering away on the streets in Norske. Legend had it their dogs even barked in Norwegian. You wanna learn about lefse? This small town in the southeastern part of the state, in bluff country, is where you want to go. It is Lefse Land.

So it was a few days before Christmas and I was hightailing it down Highway 52 on my way south from Minneapolis. The fog, *uff da*. It was so bad I could barely see my speedometer, which read sixty-five mph. There were also patches of ice on the road. I was late for an important meeting with four of Spring Grove's finest. The topic: lefse.

It was 11:15 a.m. when I parked across from The Bake Shoppe. I was fifteen minutes late, but, hey, with the fog and all, surely The Ladies of Lefse would understand. I entered the restaurant, and there they were, sitting at a round table having coffee. I smiled and said hello.

"You're late," scolded one Lady of Lefse. "We almost left."

I began to protest about the fog and the ice, when another Lady said that they were afraid of me. I was from Minneapolis and all. Indeed, Emma Landsom of the Sons of Norway, who set up this convocation, had told me on the phone that a couple of The Ladies of Lefse agreed to meet me, but only in a public place. Couldn't be too careful, you know.

"I don't want my name in the newspaper, either," snapped a third Lady of Lefse. "We're not sure we want to talk with you."

"Wait a minute," I said. "This isn't for the paper, it's for a book. And what's the harm in talking lefse?" They kinda fidgeted in their chairs and looked at each other sideways, as if to say, "Well, all right, but let's watch this one."

I pulled out my tape recorder and asked for names, which did little to put The Ladies of Lefse at ease. They looked around the restaurant to see how this was going over with others there for coffee or lunch. Then they introduced themselves. Going clockwise, Mabel Holten sat next to me to my left. Then came Inez Wilhemson, Ethel Olson, and Olga Evenmoe.

I took a deep breath and thought this was going to be a tough row to hoe. I decided to ask for recipes right away. What better way to reach out than to exchange recipes? We talked about real versus instant potatoes, powdered versus granular sugar, margarine versus butter, half and half versus whipping cream.

Inez, it turned out, made lefse for the Sons of Norway, but

not at home anymore. "It's a lot of work," she said. I asked if she missed making it. "No," she said, without hesitation. "I'm not that fond of it." Okay, I thought to myself, this was not going to be a sentimental journey down Lefse Lane.

"I love flatbread," said Olga. "I love flatbread."

"That's what you should write a story on," advised Ethel. "It's better than lefse."

I said thanks, maybe that'll be my next book. I started to wonder if things wouldn't have been different had I not been late.

Ethel explained, while the rest were writing down each other's lefse recipes, that about twenty women got together yearly and baked six hundred and fifty rounds of lefse for a big Sons of Norway holiday dinner. They did the same for Syttende Mai and for the Fall Foliage Festival in Spring Grove.

I asked if everyone loved all this lefse they made. "Some like it and some don't," said Olga, with a chuckle. "I think all Norwegians like it."

"We've got comments that it's like shoe leather," said Ethel, with a modest laugh. Well now, first a chuckle and now a laugh, things were warming up. Then reaching toward the tape recorder—but not touching it—she added, again with a laugh, "but don't put that down. Oh no. If it's good lefse, it isn't shoe leather."

"The less flour you use the better," said Mabel, and the rest agreed and discussed how many times they turn the lefse while rolling and while the lefse was on the grill. Talking shop.

"Don't you think we learn by experience?" said Ethel to a chorus of "sure, sure." "When we first started it didn't work out that well. But we kept going until we learned how to do it."

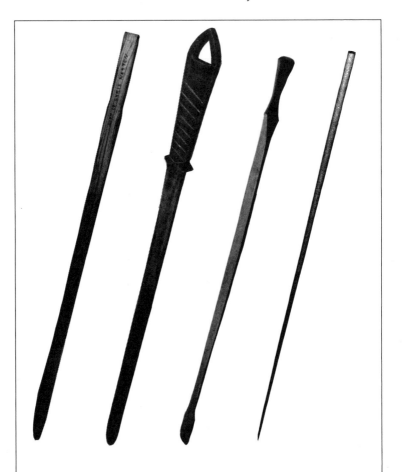

Lefse sticks were once longer, up to thirty inches. Lefse was made on stove tops or on twenty-five inch grills. With such space cooks made lefse as big as board games. To turn these monsters, you needed to walk softly and carry a big stick. (Photos by Vesterheim, The Norwegian-American Museum in Decorah, Iowa.)

You don't need a lot of fancy tools to learn, either, agreed The Ladies of Lefse. For example, you don't need to buy pricey lefse sticks; you can sand down part of a peach crate, or just yank the long sticks from window shades and shave down one end to a point. Or you don't need to buy a round board for rolling, with its own custom fitted pastry cloth. Just put the backside of an oilcloth on top the counter. "Or it works just as well with a plain corn sack," said Ethel. "You know, seed corn used to come in canvas bags. You wash that and bleach it and it gets to be a real good surface for rolling."

"Ya, you tack it on your baking board," which can be a simple piece of plywood, said Mabel.

"I can tell you this: I taught my daughter-in-law to make it, and now she outdoes me," said Ethel. "She can get hers so thin and so nice. She's really learned. She makes a lot of it."

"I think anyone can learn," said Olga.

"Oh, sure they can," said Ethel.

"If they can make lefse, they can make flatbread," added Olga.

"You and your flatbread," I said, smiling and shaking my head. Everyone laughed.

I asked if they thought lefse making was dying out. Probably not around there, they said. "But you can wonder about it," said Ethel, "because, you know, a lot of the younger ones, oh, they want to come and learn to make lefse. But when lefse-making day arrives, they never come."

"No, they don't," said Mabel.

"Like for our Syttende Mai dinners, you know," continued Ethel. "We'd like to have them come and make lefse, but they never come. I don't know if they think they are not good enough, or . . . There are so many things to learn in making lefse. It isn't just the rolling. It's the mixing and—"

"Some of the older ones don't hardly know how," said Mabel. "It's flour on the floor and flour all over the table and on their faces."

The Ladies of Lefse had all finished copying each other's recipes, and now Mabel asked me, "What's your recipe, then?"

"Uhhhh," I said, as together The Ladies of Lefse lowered their heads and prepared for my dictation. I was stunned by their request. Why would The Ladies of Lefse want *my* recipe? They must have seen scores of others. I began to realize that the recipe-exchange ritual shows respect and acceptance. I was one of them, temporarily, another lefse maker.

The Ladies of Lefse were still poised over their recipe cards, waiting for my recipe and now wondering what my problem was. I was drawing a blank, so I tried to stall. "Basically, it's potatoes . . .," I said lamely.

The Ladies of Lefse started to write down "potatoes," but when nothing else came forth, their shoulders drooped and they gave me a laugh that seemed to say: "Oh, potatoes—how interesting! Olga, this fellow from Minneapolis uses potatoes in his lefse!"

I laughed and admitted, "You guys caught me a little off guard here. I'm supposed to be the one asking the questions. Yes, I have a recipe, which I can't remember right now. It's in my van parked across the street. Lemme go get it."

I pushed my chair back to stand up, and instead of the chair sliding backward, it tipped over with a bang. The Ladies of Lefse laughed at this, but not *at* me—*with* me, as if trying to explain to the growing lunchtime crowd at The Bake Shoppe that it's okay, folks, he's from Minneapolis. Olga chuckled and said a bit loudly, "Didn't hurt anybody."

Rattled a bit, I rushed out to my van and realized I had to go back in there and face the buzzing patrons at The Bake

Shoppe. I also realized I had left my tape recorder on. Olga or Mabel—I couldn't tell which one from the tape, really, because they were sisters with similar voices—said amid the chuckles about my chair trick, "He doesn't have us intimidated, anyway."

"No," someone agreed. Then Ethel realized the recorder was still running and laughed as she pointed this out to the others. I came back into the restaurant, and The Ladies of Lefse were all laughing about their secret, which wasn't a secret because it was all on tape. Ethel explained to me that I'd have to find out what was said by listening to the tape.

"Okay, okay," I said. "Now here's my recipe." I realized this was my time, time graciously offered by The Ladies of Lefse. There was silence after I read each item, the same kind of attentive silence that's between the reading of names at a graduation ceremony.

We spent the next ten minutes or so talking lefse. We were all relaxed, chatting away. Then it was lunchtime, time for them to go. Ethel's husband, Raymond, waited at a nearby table, just in case this guy from Minneapolis had turned out to be some sort of kook. I kidded Ethel about it, and we laughed.

They left, and Olga, ever so fond of flatbread, said, "Well, thank you." Polite. Friendly.

I ordered lunch, a bit dazed, not quite sure what to make of it all. The ash tray on the table read:

"Uff Da"
Spring Grove, Minn.

10
The "Perfect" Lefse

REMEMBER, lefse makers, it's perseverance—not perfection—we want. Stick with making lefse, even when your dough always seems too sticky and your "rounds" end up looking more like a "map of the state of Texas," as Eunice Stoen of Decorah, Iowa, put it.

I drove myself mercilessly when learning to make these super thin, super round masterpieces. I was a man on a *mission*. Focused. If a masochistic drill sergeant had been passing through my kitchen during those times when I messed up and was flogging myself for it, he probably would have tipped his hat and said, "Like your style, mister."

I laugh now at how hard I was on myself then. And I laughed when I saw the section of the recipe/poem I found in the *Centennial Cook Book* by the Lutheran Church Women in Starbuck, Minnesota:

> . . . Den yew steal tree ounces of butter
> An vit two fingers pinch some salt.
> Yew beat dis [dough] wery lightly
> If it ain't gude it iss *your fault*
> [author's emphasis] . . .

Lefse making should be a no-fault affair. I discussed this a few days before Christmas with Elida Peterson of Rushford, Minnesota (pop. 1,478). Elida impressed me as a big-hearted woman who smiled easily and laughed loud. Time went fast when talking with Elida. Like many older people, she seemed not overly burdened with doubt. It was either this way or that. And, when it came to making lefse, it was *this* way.

It was early evening and she had just finished making lefse that afternoon. For Christmas that year she was giving three dozen lefse to each of her six grown children. Her place in Good Shepherd Apartments still smelled of lefse. She was selling lefse again that year at Christmas, and the phone rang as we sat at the table. Ya, she would take their order.

Even reaching up to answer the phone was hard for Elida. She had arthritis bad in her hip and had had two knee replacements. When she shifted her weight on the pillows on her chair, she just had to pause and gulp down the pain.

"I think this is going to be my last year making lefse," she said, with a sigh. "And without lefse, it won't be Christmas. I've always had lefse at Christmas. Always."

Sure it would be tough to give it up, she admitted, but what could she do? The pain, you know. The phone rang again. Ya, Mildred, but not a dozen. Elida would make her six rounds of lefse, and that would be it.

Elida sat at her table and demonstrated how she rolled, or rather, how the pin rolled. She didn't lean on the pin, which was eighty years old and belonged to her grandmother, but guided it *across* the lefse, not down into it. She said less flour went into the lefse that way, making her product tender, not tough. "I taught my daughter to roll and the first three or four went into the garbage. She was pressing so tight. You don't need to do that."

Elida herself may have been pressing a bit when she learned from her mother. "She'd stand over me with a yard-stick," said Elida with a smile and a raised eyebrow. "You didn't dare poke a hole in that lefse. You had to be careful with your stick."

Like Elida, June Olson of Starbuck, Minnesota, (pop. 1,224) also sold lefse. Perfect lefse. Lots of it. She bought eighteen hundred pounds of potatoes in the fall and maybe a hundred more in the spring and produced two thousand lefse in that time. She had sent lefse to every state except South Carolina in the sixty years she'd been making lefse, and she had worn a quarter of an inch off the ridges of her rolling pin, which came from Norway with her mother-in-law.

June was Irish and Scotch and said of lefse, "I never saw the stuff until I got married." After marrying Oliver Olson, June worked a lot in the field on the family farm fourteen miles northwest of Starbuck. She learned lefse making from her mother-in-law. "I'd make a few and take them down with dinner to the men haying in the fields," she said. "I didn't want others seeing my mistakes, and I knew the men wouldn't care. They'd eat them."

June's daughter and neighbor, Olive Voeller, was with us at June's house, helping June, now eighty, make lefse. Olive baked the lefse and stacked the finished rounds between towels, but she wouldn't roll—at least not in front of Mom. "I still hide mine," said Olive, chuckling. "I roll them all different shapes, or they get holes in them and look like a venetian blind."

I asked June if she hadn't been a bit intimidated when she was learning from her mother-in-law. "I wasn't intimidated, and she shouldn't be," June said, nodding to Olive. They

Olive Voeller, wielding a lefse stick, helped her 80-year-old mother, June Olson, make lefse. Olive baked, saying she wouldn't roll—at least not in front of Mom. "I still hide mine," said Olive, chuckling.

were both smiling and amused by my prodding.

"I just might start rolling and let her laugh at me," said Olive with a blush. My guess was that Olive could probably roll fine, but she liked making lefse with her mom, who had always rolled. There would be plenty of time for rolling after June quit. But for now they were a team, respectful and appreciative of each other.

Speaking of perfect lefse, I asked tongue-in-cheek, how about The World's Largest Lefse made right here in town in 1983 by The Boys of Starbuck? "Imagine a nine-foot lefse made by men who never make lefse," said June, shaking her head. "It wasn't bad, though. They asked me to be a part of that. I was scared to tackle something that big. We women, we wouldn't have had as much fun as those men did."

"What do you mean?" I asked.

"Women wouldn't have poked fun at each other like they did. They weren't going for perfection, for a perfect round."

Sabel Jorde of Rushford, Minnesota, was eighty-two and had been making lefse for fifty-some years. Big lefse you can drape over your forearm, yet thin enough so you can see your freckles underneath. Lefse good enough that neighbors would vie for snow-shoveling privileges, knowing they were going to get a load of lefse in return.

"Not all my lefse are so good," she said. "When I started I had some that got pretty thick." She shrugged, smiled and added, "But the kids were small and they ate them up."

Marie Kjome, of Spring Grove, Minnesota, (pop. 1,275) was taking care of a neighbor's three-month-old boy, who was fussing as we talked lefse. Marie said she liked to make lefse in the dark, still peace of four a.m. Just you and your lefse, I suppose; no distractions, no fussing children, no noise except the hum and hiss of the electric grill.

On the practical side, at four a.m., "you get a stable current and your grill stays hot," she said, bouncing the boy on one knee and then the other. "By seven a.m., everyone else is up using electricity, and your lefse doesn't get done as fast."

"Or as well?" I asked.

She waved off my question momentarily as she stood and shifted first a cloth diaper and then the wailing boy to her left shoulder. This helped. She didn't seem to have much time for perfection, and she said with a smile, "I don't make perfect rounds of lefse, but so what? They get eaten anyway." She excused herself and went to the kitchen to prepare a bottle for the baby.

Martha Mueller introduced me to her mother-in-law, Elvira Mueller, who kidded me that where she was from, over in Albert Lea, Minnesota, they used to use lefse as a sweat pad for horses. We were sitting in the parsonage kitchen. Pastor Harold Mueller was minister at Trinity Lutheran Church in Spring Grove.

"Our first parish was in Poulsbo, Washington, a Norwegian fishing village," said Martha, whose father was Norwegian and mother Swedish. "About thirty ladies would get together to make lefse for their lutefisk-and-lefse dinner. And there was a pecking order. The best lefse makers rolled, and the rest of us did other things. I only got to cool the lefse," which involved turning the finished rounds before they were stacked.

At the tenth anniversary of the opening of Spring Grove Manor, a retirement home, the Muellers were part of a crew that organized lefse making in the manor. "It was a time when people could come and roll, watch, eat, and enjoy," said Martha. "But, again, you'd see this pecking order. It was kind of sad. Some of the residents would want to try rolling but said they couldn't do it well enough. A holier-than-thou attitude can be all over lefse making, and so there can be big fears about making it."

You might guess that there was no pecking order in Martha's house when she and her children, Noel, Naomi, and Linnea, made lefse. Her children rolled when they wanted to, even if it meant a mess or thick lefse. There may have been holes in the lefse, but there was no holier-than-thou attitude in the parsonage kitchen. "You have to learn by doing, by getting the feel for it," she said.

I wish all would-be lefse makers who may be put off by this perfectionism could have learned lefse making from Anna Alden. Anna made lefse on roller skates.

True. When she wasn't rolling out a round, Anna, who died in 1961 at the age of eighty-three, would roll on her

A typical fireplace of early Norwegian-Americans. The grill rested on four-inch tripods or stones, making lefse making back-breaking labor. The round-ended tool made krumkake, and the flat-ended tool made waffles. The long-handled pan is a bed warmer. About an hour before bedtime hot coals were put in the pan, which was covered and placed under the tick, or case, of the feather mattress. The bed warmer was removed for sleeping and the kitchen fire was usually allowed to go out. This made for cozy sleeping and fast foot-work in the morning. If you weren't awake before your feet hit the floor, you were afterward. (Photos by Vesterheim, The Norwegian-American Museum in Decorah, Iowa.)

skates across the linoleum floor over to the grill or to the table in her house in north Minneapolis.

"She knew how to raise hell a little bit," said Jan Alden, Anna's granddaughter. "She wasn't your typical Norwegian. She'd dress up and put on a wig, pretending to be someone else when she answered the door. When I was a girl we moved from Minneapolis to a suburb of Los Angeles and she lived with us and took care of the kids. She'd get bored and say, 'Let's go to town.' And then she'd take us hitchhiking. We never told my mother."

It didn't sound like Anna was one to get hung up on perfect rounds of lefse. Actually, explained Jan, she didn't roller skate all the time when making lefse. See, this one time she was planning to go to a roller skating party. "She needed to practice skating, so she put on her skates and did her household chores," which included making lefse, said Jan.

I asked Jan how good was the lefse made by The Roller Skating Roller. "The lefse was fine," remembered Jan, "but you have to understand that no one liked lefse. She tried to carry on the Norwegian ways, but none of us really picked them up. We hated the lutefisk and the lefse."

Hated lefse? Hated lefse?! Lutefisk, maybe, but lefse, no.

"ISS CALLED LEFSE FOR A PURPOSE"

O Lord it iss hard to make lefse
Dat iss perfect in every vay.
To roll dem so round and so tin
Ha, ha, ha, ho, ho—*dat* vill be da day!
To know lefse, ya sure, iss to love it
No matter how tick, tough, or dead.
And if lefse vas s'pose to be yust right
Ve'd call lefse "yust rightse" instead.

11

Herb and Anna
After the Stroke

IT WAS A GRAY, damp December afternoon in Spring Grove, Minnesota, (pop. 1,275) thirteen days before Christmas. I approached the house of Herb and Anna Solum feeling frazzled from the holidays and from my trip down from Minneapolis. I was sleepy from my lunch, and in general about as fresh as a soggy sandbakkel.

In truth, part of the reason for my dragging was the dread of memories that come up whenever I am with a stroke victim. I had been told that Herb had suffered a stroke in 1989; his right side had been paralyzed and he had a loss of speech.

It reminded me of my Mom's stroke in 1974. I had been away studying at the University of Illinois. One afternoon after work, Mom, Darlene Schumacher, came home to our dairy farm near Dixon, Illinois, and dropped right there on the barn floor as my stepdad, Hank Schumacher, was milking. White floor lime all over her dress. An aneurysm had popped in her head at age forty-four.

I drove to the hospital in time to hold her hand and tell her I loved her as she lay alive but unconscious in Dixon's hospital. As I held her hand, she pulled her right leg up, as if struggling to climb out of bed.

The next day she was transferred to Rockford, Illinois, where a neurologist would do cranial surgery to repair the ruptured blood vessel. She survived surgery, but I'll never forget seeing her for the first time afterward. I turned the corner in the hospital ward, and there was this little woman, head shaved, crumpled in a wheelchair. Her glasses were crooked, and she gave me a terrifying, out-of-it look that gave no hint she knew who I was. I had lost my Mom.

But slowly, over the next few years, I got her back again. Rehabilitation, medication, and time brought her back. She never went back to work and she doesn't drive, but there's not much else she doesn't do. And her mind is all there. It could have been much worse.

I knocked on Solum's door, and I wondered how Herb and Anna were adjusting in those most difficult first few years after a stroke. For some reason, I wondered about the smell of the house. No, I was not concerned about the house being clean, but I remember a yellow staleness in the air when I'd call on Mom and Hank right after the stroke. Things were too close, too still, too boarded up. It was the smell of clothes that just hang in the closet unused, season after season. It was the smell of old photo albums that Mom would open when I'd come. She'd touch each still-bright black and white, as if re-affirming she was once that girl or that bride or that mother holding her baby. It was the smell of sadness.

Anna came to the door, trim and smiling. She opened the door and—swoosh—the unmistakable smell of fresh lefse. Yes, she said, they (did she say "they," Anna *and* Herb?) had just made lefse that morning. I didn't see Herb. Maybe he was resting.

We sat at the kitchen table and began talking lefse. Herb's mother, Marie Solum, used to sell lefse. People from all around would call on her during the holidays, hoping she could make them an order of lefse. Usually, she said, sure, pick up your order on such-and-such a date. Lefse wasn't in the stores in the '40s and '50s, said Anna.

Could you stay for some coffee, Marie would ask when customers arrived for their lefse. "She was a widow," said Anna, "and she lived alone. Making lefse was a good thing for her. It made her feel useful and happy when people would stay and talk."

Anna added that it was hard on Marie when the health inspector shut her down; it seems Marie had an open stairway in the kitchen, which, for some such reason, wasn't allowed in buildings that sold goods.

Anna said her children, Patricia Solum Hill and Richard Solum, "craved" lefse when they were kids, and Grandma kept the family stocked. But after Grandma died in 1971, the heat was on Herb and Anna to start laying in their own lefse. "Herb was always bossing me to learn to make lefse," said Anna, clearly fond of this memory. Anna wasn't so sure; making lefse was a lot of work and there was a trick to it. And Anna had a back that acted up from time to time.

"So, finally, Herb says, 'Okay, we'll both do it. You get the grill, but we're going to use Mrs. Ida Sacquitne's recipe.'" For years Mrs. Sacquitne was generally believed to be the most notable lefse maker in the land; she had made lefse for King Olav V of Norway on a visit to Decorah and had been flown to the Smithsonian in Washington, D.C., to make lefse for the Bicentennial in 1976.

Anna got Mrs. Sacquitne's recipe, "but then we couldn't find a grill," she said. "So Herb bought a new grill" and they had a go at making their first lefse together—a joint project.

Potatoes were mashed in kettles by these objects of art. Most potato mashers were not as beautiful as the "horse-hoof" model (upper left). (Photos by Vesterheim, The Norwegian-American Museum in Decorah, Iowa.)

"Well, I wish I had a movie camera around then. Flour everywhere, and the lefse weren't at all round. They were an awful shape; I don't know how to explain it. And then the lefse would stick and fall apart as we tried to get it to the grill. We were thinking that here we had invested in all these lefse-making tools, and it turned out like this. Let me tell you, we should have had Grandma Solum here."

To their credit, they kept at it and improved, Herb and Anna did. Anna would roll the lefse and Herb would bake them.

(It is my belief that Lena, the Goddess of Lefse, purposely conducts bootcamp in the bakery by bedeviling all beginning lefse makers. So, beginners, don't take it personally. All good lefse makers who have gone on to do masterpiece work have had their first failures—and they recount them with pride.)

"When we make lefse now, it's tough," said Anna. "Last year [the first Christmas after the stroke] when we made lefse, he sat right there and cried. Stroke victims cry so easily, you know. It was awful.

"Lefse making was one of the things we really clicked on together. Sometimes married couples don't click, but Herb and I were a darn good team. He got the griddle ready, and I would roll out the lefse and put them on the griddle for him to bake. We'd pass the lefse stick back and forth between us.

"But he can still boss me, though. Now this morning, Herb finally was able to take the lefse off the griddle, and he worked the flour into the dough. Today, he didn't cry. So, you know . . ." Her voice trailed off but her tone was hopeful.

"Now, do you want some lefse?" she asked in a peppy way.

"Never thought you'd ask," I said, grinning. Anna buttered and put sugar on several lefse and then announced in a silly-me manner that she was out of coffee. I'd manage, I said, as I wolfed down my third piece.

"How's the lefse?" she asked me. I said it was great, and she was genuinely relieved and flattered.

As I put on my coat to go, I asked if Herb was resting. No, it seemed it would take more than a stroke to keep ol' Herb down. He was over at the log cabin/public library playing euchre. I chuckled. I wouldn't be surprised, I thought, if one of these Christmases real soon Herb and Anna once again passed the lefse stick back and forth to each other.

12
The Grand
Ol' Lady of Lefse

I HAD AVOIDED making this call to Ida Sacquitne. Ida the
Great, the legendary lefse maker from Decorah, Iowa
(pop. 8,063). I held the telephone receiver in my hand,
hesitant to punch out Ida's phone number, and I remembered what Anna Solum from Spring Grove, Minnesota,
had told me; that years ago when she and Herb finally made
the commitment to learn lefse making, Herb had insisted
that they use the recipe of Ida Sacquitne.

I remembered the recipe that Ethel Olson, also of Spring
Grove, quoted to me that morning at The Bake Shoppe: the
recipe of Ida Sacquitne.

I remembered the name of the woman who thirty years
ago had taught Eunice Stoen, lefse-maker supreme of
Decorah, to make lefse: Ida Sacquitne.

I remembered sitting in the Dayton House, a Norwegian
restaurant in Decorah, and asking the waitress if, by chance,
she had ever heard of anyone by the name of Ida . . . (I
didn't even get the Sacquitne out of my mouth.) The waitress said the surname for me, and said, "Sure, everyone
knows Ida. Good lefse."

*Ida the Great. During the Bicentennial the Smithsonian Institute
in Washington, D.C., declared Ida Sacquitne "a national
American treasure for her skills in Norwegian-American
cooking." She had made lefse for the King of Norway, and,
at age ninety, she was still rolling strong. (Photos of Ida
by Sarah Fromm, The Decorah Newspapers.)*

And I remembered the first time I heard the name. Dr.
Marion Nelson, director of Vesterheim, insisted I talk with
someone named Ida Sacquitne. He had to spell her name a
couple times for me. Uh-huh, I said, what's so special
about . . . I couldn't pronounce Sacquitne (it's Sock-
whitney).

Well, he said, not knowing where to begin, Ida had demonstrated lefse making at Nordic Fest. During the Bicentennial in 1976, Ida made lefse at the Smithsonian in Washington, D.C. She had made lefse for Norway's King Olav V, and if that wasn't enough, Ida Sacquitne was quite a character.

And now, I was going to call her to see if she'd demonstrate lefse making for me. Gary WHO?, she'd probably say. From WHERE? You want me to make lefse for you WHEN? TOMORROW!

Wait, I said to myself, she probably didn't even answer her phone anymore. All calls were probably screened by a secretary, who would direct me to Ida's agent, who would say in a take-it-or-leave-it fashion that she could give me ten minutes with Ida . . . let's see . . . in three weeks.

What the heck, I said finally, let's just give it a go. Dial her up, or her secretary, or agent, or whomever, and maybe they'll succumb to the Christmas spirit and give me an audience with Ida the Great.

The phone started ringing and I told myself that it was a couple weeks before Christmas and people in Decorah just had to be deep in the holiday mood.

"Hello?"

Odd, I thought. Usually secretaries or agents identify themselves and say something like, "May I help you?" Somewhat tentatively, I said that I was trying to reach Ida— and then my mouth froze up and I just could not spit out Sacquitne. Oh brother, I thought, there goes my audience right there.

"—Sacquitne." The women at the other end said the name and got me off the hook.

"Yes, Ida Sac—Yes, is Ida there?" I managed to ask.

"Yeah."

There was quiet at the other end of the line. No putting-me-on-hold music or setting down of the receiver followed by background commotion as someone fetched Ida. Suddenly, I realized I just might be talking to Ida herself. "Ida? Is this Ida?" No, it couldn't be, I thought.

"Yeah," she said in a how-many-times-do-I-have-to-tell-you tone of voice.

I tried to compose myself and explained that I was writing a book on lefse and—

"On *what?*" she interrupted.

"On lefse," I replied, and she made a nasal kind of noise that said: Now if that don't beat all. But I sensed she was starting to smile. I went on to say that I had heard a lot about her and I would like to watch her make lefse.

"When?"

"Uh, well, how about tomorrow?" I looked at my watch and winced: You bonehead, Gary, it was nearly nine p.m. Sure Ida the Great was going to stay up that night and make dough so some stranger from Minneapolis could watch a lefse-making demo.

"Well, I suppose that will be okay," she said. "I'm going to be making my last batch for Christmas tomorrow morning anyway. You come down."

I was shocked and started to blubber on about how grateful I was and how I had heard so much about her. "Ya, ya," she cut me short. "See you at ten." And she hung up.

It was a beautiful Christmas-season morning, so sunny that even dark sunglasses couldn't smooth out a hard squint. I was cruising down Highway 52, listening to the radio and humming holiday carols. "It's a marshmallow world in the winter, a marshmallow world that is grand." East of Harmony, Minnesota, just before turning south and crossing into Iowa, I saw Amish people riding on the shoulder of the road in a black carriage, pulled by a black horse puffing steam out its nose.

I reached Decorah and looked for Ida's street. I had a hard time finding it and pulled up to a pickup truck parked by the post office. I asked the driver about the street in question. He directed me, and asked who I was looking for. Ida Sacquitne, I said. Oh yeah, Ida lives right over there, he said.

I drove to her place, a twenty-four-unit retirement home called Heritage Haven, and walked into the lobby. An elderly woman wearing an apron was standing there, arms down and relaxed. Her fingers were floured and slightly spread so as not to touch, and her hands were turned out in a graceful, receptive way. It was the stance common to all people at home and at peace in the kitchen. She said, "Are you the fellow from Minneapolis, then?"

"Yes. And you must be Ida."

We turned and walked toward her apartment. I was smelling lefse even from there in the hall. Her door was left open—all the women in Heritage Haven knew each other and seemed to be in each other's business—and we entered. Her kitchen was small. Ida had been rolling her lefse on a two-person table. A round was laying there from before I came. Her grill spanned the right compartment of the nearby kitchen sink. The grill was not exactly level, but it would do.

"How much flour do you use in yours?" she asked.

Ida was asking *me* about my recipe? I said about one and a quarter cups for three cups of potatoes. She said she supposed that would do. I asked her for her recipe. She started to give it: four cups potatoes, about two cups flour . . . and then, "Ah, shoot," she said. The round that had been sitting there while she went to retrieve me in the lobby had stuck and torn. "Oh well," she said, and she took a paring knife to scrape up the smudge and then rolled out the round again.

"You use two rollers," I observed.

"Oh yeah. I use this here first, with a sock on it" she said, lifting a smooth rolling pin, "and then I finish it with this," the ridged lefse pin *sans* sock. "I learned something about that in Waterloo. A woman was doing some rolling out of pie crusts, and she used two pins. And I thought to myself, 'I'm going to go hóme and do that with my lefse!' And I've done it ever since. It's easier to push them out with the smooth one, you know."

Ida couldn't quite get this round of lefse that stuck the first time to behave any better this time around. She mumbled to herself, "I guess I didn't use enough flour. Ah well." She lifted the reluctant round up, finally, turned toward the sink and put it onto the grill. She said she liked to add salt to her recipe. How much, I asked. "Salt? Oh, I don't know," she said with a shrug. A dash, I suggested. "Sounds good. Same with sugar," she said.

"Anything else?" I asked. "Any cream?"

"Oh ya, I use some half and half. I use, oh, I use two tablespoons of margarine at least, and then I pour some half and half in. I don't know, two, three tablespoons?"

I chuckled to myself, thinking of all the perfectionism that has gotten pulled into lefse making over the years. Ida's attitude of a little of this, a little of that was so refreshing.

She rolled out another one. "You turn your round once, and then finish rolling it out. Why?" I asked.

"I don't know. I've gotten in the habit of doing it, I guess."

She finished rolling and used her stick to lift the lefse to the grill. In the process, a hole emerged. "Oh yeah, you get those, sometimes."

She told me to try rolling out one with the smooth pin. I was surprised that I wasn't intimidated; Ida was just easy

Lefse was commonly baked on the top grill, a twenty-five inch flat iron plate. The fourteen-inch cast iron grills (bottom two) made potetlamp, a thick lefse. Dr. Marion Nelson, director of Vesterheim Museum, said many people made lefse on woodburning stoves. "I remember my mother scouring down the top of the stove for lefse baking," he recalled. (Photos by Vesterheim, The Norwegian-American Museum in Decorah, Iowa.)

to be around, I guess. However, as I was sizing up my opposition, this little ball of dough, I cleared my throat and mumbled, "I, ah, make less than perfect rounds, so . . ." I rolled the dough out some with the smooth pin.

"Now turn it over and see what we got," she said. I did, and then rolled on. "You can press a little harder with that pin, now. Ya, you can, you know. Now, you can finish it with this." She handed me the lefse pin, which was an old one with fixed handles, different from mine with handles that stay stationary in the hand while the pin rolls. The smoothed handles felt good in my hands.

"You're doing a pretty good job," she told me.

Ida had been so attentive to me that she—we—had forgotten about the one on the grill. "Oh, God," she said as she spied the blackened round on the grill, edges all curled. "Gee, I forgot about this one. This one's for the dog."

I told her I had probably been distracting her. She waved her hand: Ah, no big deal. I asked how long she grills the first side. "Till it starts to bubble. That's what my aunt told me."

Ida told me to try it again, rolling with two pins. Then she showed me how to fold the finished rounds; in half, and then in half again. The folded rounds were triangular now and were stacked so the pointed corner and straight edges were always outside; the jagged third side was always inside. This softened up the edges that could go dry. "But then you got to open up every one again before you sell them," she added. "If you freeze them this way they stick together."

I had always used two sticks to pick up my rolled-out lefse, but peer pressure was getting to me and, at my request, Ida showed me how to pick them up with one stick. Flip an edge over the stick and wrap the round around the stick by rolling

After showing me her two-pin rolling method and her one-stick turning technique, Ida had me roll a few rounds. Then she said, "You know, there's a dinky little one here for you to eat."

the stick toward the middle, she said. Pick it up and put it on the grill by reversing the process.

"You know, there's a dinky little one here for you to eat," she said. Dinky or not, it tasted real gude, as they say.

A woman from Meals-on-Wheels came in and left lunch for Ida, who started talking about her family. Her husband, Myer, a farmer, was dead, and two of her six children had died. She had "over twenty great grandchildren and over twenty grandchildren, so I've got a pile of them. I'm rich. I think that's good," she said, nodding to me to take the done lefse off the grill.

We started talking about her trip to the Smithsonian. I asked how it came about that she went. "Well, there was somebody that came to the museum [Vesterheim] and he said to . . . oh, what is his name . . . ya, Marion Nelson, he said, 'We have to have somebody who could make something [at the Bicentennial celebration],' " Ida said. " 'Well, I know. We can get Ida to make some lefse.'

"So Marion Nelson he sent this guy up to me. I took out some lefse and showed him how I rolled. 'Well, I think maybe you're going to get to go to Washington,' he said. 'Would you go?'

"I said, 'Yes, I'll go.' And a lot of friends said, 'Aren't you scared?' 'Scared? Scared of what?' "

I asked about the time she made lefse for the King of Norway, when he visited Vesterheim in 1987. Did she say anything when the king entered the room in which Ida was rolling? "What did I say? Oh I said, *Her kommer han.* That's 'Here he comes' in Norwegian. Then he laughed. He knew I could talk Norwegian. Then he bragged about how it was wonderful that I could do that good thing [make lefse.]"

Ida fetched some clippings about her lefse making. One clipping said Ida was eighty-six when the King came. It suddenly dawned on me, as Ida moved to find more clippings and pictures, that Ida was old. Not old as in worn out, but old as in enduring, venerable. I asked her age. She said she would be ninety in July. Whew, ninety and still rolling lefse. It occurred to me Ida was not that much younger than Grandma Legwold would have been had she not died.

I skimmed through more clippings. "Says here you were declared a national American treasure?" I asked, somewhat surprised and very impressed.

She chuckled. "A treasure," she said in a such-silliness tone of voice. Then it hit her. "A what? For lefse?"

I quoted from the newspaper article: " 'In 1976 the Smithsonian Institute declared Ida a national American treasure for her skills in Norwegian-American cooking.' "

"Oh ya, I s'pose," she said. "Lefse doesn't mean so much to me, you know; it's so common. It's fun to give it away. Why? Because they like it, I s'pose. Here, there are twenty-four units. Course that one didn't want it. She says, [Ida here used a mock-scolding voice] 'I don't eat lefse. Get out of here!' But she's a bit queer." Ida had a good laugh at that.

"All the rest of the units, I've given them each two lefse. I told them they could freeze them for Christmas if they wanted to save them."

I asked Ida if she envisioned the day when she'd no longer be able to make lefse for Christmas.

"Ah, I don't know. As long as I can drag my stuff down here, I can make them, I s'pose."

Ida's lunch was getting cold, and it was time to go. She walked me out to the lobby and gossiped a little about the

13

A Lefse in Every Lean-to

MERLIN HOINESS, aka Mr. Lefse, had a vision for lefse. He could see—maybe someday—this Scandinavian holiday food becoming a year-round household staple, whether you're Norske or not.

It was a few days before Christmas and I'd come down to the snow-covered bluff country, Rushford, Minnesota, (pop. 1,478) to talk lefse with Mr. Lefse himself. He was buying me lunch at the Mill Street Inn, where the regulars were playing euchre in the corner booths. Merlin was not a wild-eyed evangelist about lefse, but it was clear he'd given lefse some thought.

"You know, ten, twelve years ago you couldn't sell tortillas," said Merlin, who had been in the grocery business in nearby Harmony, Minnesota, (pop. 1,133) all his life. "They had to be promoted. You can do that with lefse, too."

"Even to people who aren't Scandinavian?" I asked, playing devil's advocate.

"Oh, I get some Germans who come up to me and say: 'I'm German. I don't eat that stuff.'" he said. "You know what my reaction is to that? I tell them to try a bratwurst in lefse. Everybody likes lefse. Kids love it; they won't eat potatoes at home, but they take one bite of lefse and they get a big smile. They can't get enough of it. You know, Zola [Merlin's wife] and I do these lefse-making demonstrations this time of year, but with Easter, and Syttende Mai, and all these festivals and lutefisk dinners and such, we could do demonstrations every week out of the year.

"The future is coming for lefse. The market is out there. I mean, people this time of year want it bad—they'll eat it even when it's green. Yeah, the last ten years ethnic food has jumped in popularity. My belief is people want to go back to their base again."

I had first met Merlin and Zola a week earlier up in the Twin Cities at Lyngblomsten Care Center for the elderly in St. Paul. They did their lefse demo at a Christmas party for the residents. Zola rolled and grilled lefse, and Merlin, wearing an apron that said "Take A Liking to Viking Mat" (Food), prepared samples—some plain, some with butter and sugar, some with butter and brown sugar, and some with sour cream and ham. He also sold a fun little book he had written, *91 Ways To Serve Lefse*, as well as packages of lefse made by Zola or by Norsland Kitchens in Rushford. A video-tape of how lefse was made at Norsland played continuously during the demo.

Merlin started Norsland Kitchens in 1981 in Harmony, moved it to Rushford in 1987, and had recently sold most of his interest in the lefse-making factory.

Amid all the hubbub at Lyngblomsten's that day, Merlin greeted me by saying he had met my cousin, Denny Bengtson, the day before down in Wanamingo, Minnesota, where he and Zola did a demo. He's constantly meeting people doing this, he said. And indeed, people, some with canes or in wheelchairs and some hunched over with osteoporosis or arthritis, were at times three deep in a crush around the table, which, I noticed, was elevated by wood blocks taped to the feet. Smart, I said to myself. Save your backs that way.

People were oohing and aahing about the smell or taste of lefse—"Try the one with sour cream and ham!"—or asking Zola how she could roll so long and so well. Since lefse making is often a church function, many of the people talked about news at this church or that, or who was minister here and there. Often they reminisced about days on the farm when monstrous lefses were grilled on the range, a wood-burning cookstove. They told tales about their families, themselves, their Christmases past.

"People love to watch lefse being made," said Merlin. "It is something from their past, when their mothers and grand-mothers would make it, especially at the holidays. I know my mother would have leftover potatoes every day, which she didn't want to throw away. So she'd make lefse, and I remember having it as a kid coming home from school."

As the time wore on, a major problem developed: demand high, supply low. Merlin had underestimated how much dough to bring. While Merlin was starting to tear down the show, Zola stayed at the grill filling order after order after order. And people were still coming in, nervously clutching their dollar bills and becoming keenly aware of who was next and how much dough was left.

Norma West, a Lyngblomsten volunteer who was taking the money for the orders, had her hands full assuring the remaining residents that they would get theirs. Norma suggested we bar the doors. I smiled, thinking she was kidding. Her expression said she was dead serious. Everything eventually worked out, but as Merlin joked when we met the next week again in Rushford, "We were lucky to get out of there alive."

"HERE'S WHAT YOU DO WITH LEFSE"

Use lefse as a shingle or
As chaps if you're a cowpoke.
You want a saddle blanket then?
Try lefse . . . just a small joke.

What else? How 'bout as napkins or
As tire patches, too?
A bath mat made of lefse, though,
Is soon to turn to goo.

Lefse makes some nice diplomas.
As sheepskins, they would do.
If just Norwegians got them, though,
Who *would* you give them to?

It's just like toilet paper, but
That's simply lacking taste.
I say to those who make this claim:
"Lefse surely ain't for waste!"

Don't use it as a handkerchief
No, lefse wouldn't do.
To those who say that this is done
Just say that that snot true.

Alas, we've had some fun here and
You have to know it's so.
The only use for lefse is
For eating, don't ya know.

We finished lunch at the Mill Street Inn and ordered pie. Merlin said that the day before he had been interviewed by a reporter from the *St. Paul Pioneer Press*. Oh yeah, he said, he had had articles written about him and lefse in the local paper, *The Tri-County Record*, and in *Mpls./St. Paul* magazine. A Twin Cities TV station once sent a crew down for a feature, and he had made lefse for the assembled Minnesota Legislature and for a group of Wisconsin state senators down in Madison.

It had always been like that, he said; people were drawn to lefse. "I've been in the grocery business all my life," said Merlin, "and I could never keep the people satisfied when it came to lefse. This was before factories were making much lefse. There was a plant over in Blair, Wisconsin, but in my store I would use the lefse made by ladies in town and on the farms.

"I was actually bootlegging lefse, you see. These ladies weren't checked out by the public health inspector. He'd come into the store and ask who made my lefse. Then he'd have to take it off the shelf and throw it in the garbage."

Finally, in 1981 Merlin decided it was time to stop fighting with suppliers and health inspectors and to open Norsland Kitchens. He was delivering Norsland lefse to one hundred sixty-seven stores by 1985, when he had a heart attack and then by-pass surgery. Eventually, he sold out to Al Spande, but the two were still working together and Merlin had retained a small share of the business.

We finished our pie and coffee. Merlin paid and we headed down the street toward Norsland. I looked back at a hand-printed sign in the window of the Mill Street Inn that was touting a lutefisk-and-lefse dinner. Meanwhile, Merlin started telling me about one of the best things he did for his lefse business before he sold. In 1983, he ran a small ad in the *Billings* (Montana) *Gazette*, of all places: five packages lefse, $11.99 postage paid. He ran the ad on Thursday and by Tuesday he had twenty-four orders, the first from a Mr. Hernandez of Cody, Wyoming. With each package mailed, Merlin enclosed an order form. The address on those order forms must have been passed around a lot, because the lefse mail order business had been booming—twenty to twenty-five thousand rounds of lefse were mailed each year—and the Billings ad had been the only one Merlin had run.

We pulled into Norsland Kitchen and the place was a riot with lefse making. Behind the glass wall, conveyer belts were moving rows of rounds. Nine rolling machines, made by Jim Humble right there in Rushford, were automatically rolling, then turning the rounds and rolling and turning again and again—about thirty-six passes per round—until the rounds were seventeen inches in diameter; they shrank down to fourteen inches by the time they were grilled.

A woman with flour-covered eyelashes lifted the rolled-out lefse onto one of the half dozen gas ranges that were blazing away in blue. One baker was turning and checking and flipping the rounds, and then feeding the finished ones onto an eighty-five-foot cooling conveyer. In the back, a woman was sealing the cooled rounds in a plastic bag filled with nitrogen gas, which retarded spoiling but didn't affect taste, Merlin said. That way you didn't have to add preservatives.

Back farther in another room was a potato peeler that, basically, looked like a big bowl with the insides covered with metallic sandpaper. This rough surface rubs off the skins of a hundred pounds of spuds—in three minutes flat. Next to it was a steam cooker that cooked three hundred pounds of potatoes in forty minutes.

I met a beleaguered Al Spande, who had been back in the cooler with tomorrow's dough. Said we could talk later.

Good enough, I yelled. The automatic rolling pins noisily pounded out a surprisingly near-perfect round. Al's delivery man was on the phone: "Yeah, do me a favor, will ya? Don't push 'em. If they ask, move them out, but don't push. We're running short."

Customers were coming in to pick up their orders. Al gave them a smile. Meeting the customers was the fun part of his job. Here you go. Merry Christmas. A table against the wall was groaning with packages stacked, what, maybe ten or twelve high. Exporting lefse. I nosed around, checking labels. The lefse was bound for destinations such as the following: Colombia, MD; Bedford, MA; Manlius, NY; Newton Square, PA; Grand Prairie, TX; Scottsdale, AZ; Shreveport, LA; Houston, TX; Des Plaines, IL; Ogden, UT; Modesto, CA; Poway, CA; Fairway, KS; Sun City West, AZ; Wauwatosa, WI; Santa Paula, CA; Milwaukee, WI; Colorado Springs, CO; Ben Wheeler, TX; Owings, MD; Prairie Village, KS; Glendora, CA; Honolulu, HA.

This lefse-making commotion went on for a while, and Merlin came back up front and said, "Dolores back there says she knows your Dad."

"Really?" I was more than a little surprised. Merlin took me back and introduced me to Dolores Rude Humble. Before she married Ray Humble, she grew up with my Dad, Conrad Legwold, in Peterson, Minnesota, just five miles west of Rushford on Highway 16. Dad used to work on the North Prairie farm of Ray's brother-in-law, Arvid Kjos. Small world. Dolores asked how Dad was doing. "Fine. I'll call him tonight and tell him we met."

"Do that," she said.

It was four p.m., quitting time. I asked how many they rolled that day, as Al's five workers filed out the door: two thousand one hundred and ninety-five.

Al and I went across the street to Stumpy's for some chili and a Coke, his late lunch. I was still full from lunch at the Mill Street Inn. Al was bushed, but satisfied. He said they produced two hundred fifty to three hundred thousand rounds a year, "but fifty percent of our annual sales are in the three days before Thanksgiving and the three days before Christmas." In the holiday season, the phone rang off the hook, but come May, June, and July they shut down, he said.

Al was enthusiastic about lefse, but he left the fervor to Merlin. Al was a realist: Lefse would not follow in the wake of the tortilla and move across cultures with commercial abandon. It'd be nice, but no way.

I suggested that much of the appeal of lefse was that you *couldn't* get it everywhere, that much of it was made by the grandmother you love dearly. I wondered aloud whether factories like Norsland didn't contribute to the dying off of lefse-making. That is, people could think: "I won't make lefse this Christmas; I'll buy it instead."

The reality was lefse making wasn't going to die off, said Al. More women had to work, which meant less time for lefse making. Some older people couldn't make lefse anymore, or they had moved away to where they didn't have friends who gathered at Christmas to make lefse making fun. It was nice to know they could still get good lefse at places like Norsland, he said.

Final point: Norsland didn't want to position itself as competing with grandparents. "I like to think we're Number Two, next to Grandma's," said Al.

Al had finished eating and needed to go back to Norsland to close up. I went along, found Merlin, and thanked him for everything. Al gave me a package of fresh lefse for my trip home and for my kids, Ben and Kate. Before I left, Merlin wanted to show me a ringer-like lefse roller his father,

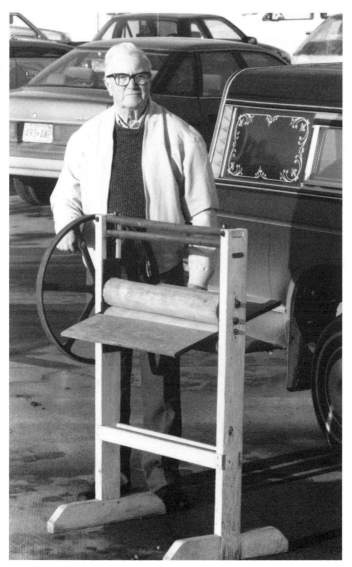

Merlin Hoiness still had a ringer-like lefse roller his father,
Edward Hoiness, had made for Merlin's mother, Jane.
She didn't like it, and so it was never used.

Edward Hoiness, had made for Merlin's mother, Jane. Took a lot of time and effort to make, he said, only his mother didn't like it much and it never got used. Oh well.

"Thanks again, guys," I said. "Merry Christmas."

Now I was hungry and I walked across the street to Stumpy's again. I ate some soup, and thought about my day. It was dark outside, and it would be a long drive back. I asked the waitress to please put some butter and sugar in little containers. Oh, and a little plastic knife—all to go.

I paid the bill and climbed into my van. It was cold. Cold and dark, and I've got "miles to go before I sleep," as Frost said. I started the engine and let it run. Maybe by the time I buttered and put sugar on one of Norsland's lefse, I'd be able to coax a little heat from my heater. If not, I thought, this lefse should heat me up from the inside.

I took a big bite out of my lefse and headed north on Highway 43. Nightfall showed off two huge lighted Christmas trees on the bluffs at the opposite ends of town.

The trees were not really trees. This morning on my way into town, I had seen that they were ornamental lights strung to look like Christmas trees. They were illusions, but welcomed ones. The blessing of darkness is that it can close our eyes but open our minds. Now at night these "trees" dared me to drop my adult thinking, for a little while, and pretend, as all kids do at Christmas. Who did I want to be? How about a cowboy riding Old Blue, my horse, through moonlit snowdrifts? Been on a cattle drive, and hadn't seen family for four long months. Blue and I reached the top of the bluff, both tired to the bone. There. Over yonder I could see light from the old kitchen. Was that the wind or were those carols I was hearing?

Yeah, it was Christmas in Minnesota and I was going home.

14

Lefse
Warms You
Twice

For the Christmas Eve family gathering one year, a three-car caravan of fools made the seventy-mile trip from the Twin Cities to the home of my cousin, Denny Bengtson, in Wanamingo, Minnesota, near Rochester. The trip was made in a snow storm with a wind chill that would slow down even Will Steger's huskies: -87° Fahrenheit.

We made it to Wanamingo okay, but the wind-whipped snow looked like thick smoke on what we could see of Highway 52. Drifts were building up fast while we ate our Christmas meal, opened presents, and sang carols, but you could tell by the glances out the window and the tense pauses in conversations that we were pre-occupied with the return trip.

We should have stayed in Wanamingo that night, but at about 7:30 p.m. we all bundled up, piled into our cars, and took off into the black howl.

We made it, oh, maybe three-tenths of a mile when Darroll Bengtson, in the lead, plowed his car—with front-wheel drive—into a tidal wave of snow that had drifted over the road going up hill. Everyone in all three cars sat and stared out the window, hoping that what we were witnessing wasn't really happening. Finally, Steve and Dick Bengtson, in the car behind me, rapped on my window and shouted the obvious: "We gotta dig Darroll out."

I thought, "Oh, for a little lefse to throw under the tires."

Well, we got Darroll out, making quick work of it because that was the best way to stay warm. I still remember getting back into the car and thinking, "Gee, I'm not so cold." I had worn a hooded parka made with three pounds of down. Then I realized I couldn't feel my legs. Numb. After a minute or so there was some tingling, and then a burning, as the thaw progressed down my legs.

Looking back, that was the Christmas that had rekindled my hopes of ever making respectable rounds of lefse. That was the year Linda Bengtson, Denny's wife, gave lefse as a gift, which inspired me to keep at lefse making until I got it right.

Last Christmas Linda gave me another gift. She had called and said they were planning a Minnesota Christmas Eve meal in Wanamingo; you know, food that was typical of Minnesota. She was making turkey, Dick and Cathy Bengtson from Grand Rapids were bringing a wild rice dish, that kind of thing. Linda wanted to know if I would make the lefse.

I was touched. Linda, you recall, had been my lefse-making mentor/therapist. Well, now, Linda was asking *me* to make lefse for Christmas Eve. What a gift.

I brought my lefse and it passed inspection. That is, people ate it up and even complimented me. One of my prouder moments.

When dinner was over, all nineteen of us moved into the living room to sing carols and open presents, squeezing together on couches or kicking off our shoes and sitting on the floor. Linda and Denny called their kids, Nathan and Brianna, up to the piano and announced that the following lefse song came home from school. They said I especially would be interested in the song, because of my lefse book. They didn't know who wrote it, but I had seen a version of the song in Red Stangland's *Norwegian Home Companion*.

When they finished singing, I applauded and asked for a copy of the lyrics. Then I wondered again, as I had wondered when visiting with all the lefse makers I had met, why do people sing songs and write poems about lefse, of all things? Taste and tradition are two major reasons, I had come to learn. But I had also learned that the most powerful reason was just as Kathy Weflen, of St. Paul, had said over breakfast one winter morning: "I never felt like I was alone while making lefse."

Lefse evokes such strong memories. Memories of the old days—of the old country or the old farmstead, perhaps. More importantly, lefse evokes memories of loved ones, those who were left behind and those who have left home. And, of course, those who have passed on. How we treasure our smooth-handle heirloom rolling pins and smudged lefse recipe cards signed "Mom" or "Grandma" or "Aunt Ethel."

I remember Mary, my sister. Lefse was the last gift I gave her before she died. I hadn't seen her for maybe ten years, but she came up to Minneapolis for Kate's baptism. It was good to see her, give her a hug. We had been so far out of touch and had not realized how much we missed each other. After the festivities were over and she was getting into her car, she asked, "Oh, by the way, what is that stuff Grandma

"THE LEFSE SONG"

(Sung to the tune of "Camptown Races")
Norsky ladies sing this song, Uff Da. Uff Da.
Bake that lefse all day long, all the Uff Da day.
Bake it till it's almost brown, Uff Da. Uff Da.
Makes you jump just like a clown, all day Uff Da day.

(chorus)
Gonna bake all night, gonna bake all day.
I'll spend my money on spuds and flour
To have me an Uff Da day.

Went downtown for some lutefisk, Uff Da. Uff Da.
De vedder vas so cold and brisk, all da Uff Da day.
Used my lefse for a Mackinaw, Uff Da. Uff Da.
Greatest yacket I ever saw
Lefse saved the day.

(chorus)
Went to town in my model T, Uff Da. Uff Da.
Tire went flat and I said, "Poor Me." It was an Uff Da day.
Used that lefse for a tire patch, Uff Da. Uff Da.
Now I gotta bake me another batch, all the Uff Da day.

(chorus)

Last winter I lost my underwear, Uff Da. Uff Da.
But this Norwegian didn't care, all the Uff Da day.
Sewed some lefse into BVDs, Uff Da. Uff Da.
Fixed me up so I didn't freeze, it was an Uff Da day.

(chorus)

Then they asked me how to spell relief, Uff Da. Uff Da.
I told them lefse saves me grief, all the Uff Da day.
Don't use Rolaids or Di-gel, Uff Da. Uff Da.
Just give me lefse and I'll get well, any old Uff Da day.

(chorus)

used to make, that flat potato stuff?"

"Oh, you mean lefse," I said.

"Yeah. Where can I get some of that? Do they sell it in stores?"

"Yeah. But let me make you some for your birthday," I said.

I've often wondered what made Mary ask for lefse, after all those years of not even hearing the word. Who knows? Maybe it was the taste, but I think it was more a matter of lefse's touch and taste and smell having the ability to take people back momentarily, usually to a simpler time, a time of warmth and love and assurance that, "There, there, it's going to be okay. Have some lefse."

I made Mary that batch, as promised. I put some rounds in a plastic Ziplock bag and sent it off Federal Express. Got there fine, and Mom recalled Mary eating it up. "The whole batch was gone in a day," said Mom with a chuckle.

I've always felt lefse warms you twice: once when you make it and again when you eat it. The warmth is in the memories, mostly, and in knowing you are never alone.

"NEVER ALONE"

Never alone and seldom sad,
The life of a lefse maker isn't so bad.

The Christmas Potatoes

A HOLIDAY SKIT

THIS LEFSE STORY was read a few years back at a family Christmas gathering. I wrote it because I was tired of Christmases of just food and small talk and presents. "The Christmas Potatoes" was a hit because of the story and because of the fun in hearing certain "aw-shucks" aunts and uncles and cousins warm up to their parts, then read lines with gusto. It's a twenty-minute skit with a narrator and six parts, three men and three women. Try reading "The Christmas Potatoes" at your next holiday gathering.

□ □ □

Each Christmas season I, Christopher the Christmas Pot Holder III, like my father and grandfather before me, am hung on the kitchen wall for decoration. I'm bright red and green with a clever design of Santa Claus dancing around the Christmas tree.

Like others who spend their time hanging around, I watch. I keep to my own business, mind you. But I cannot help it if I . . . ahem . . . notice things.

Anyway, I've noticed how neglected potatoes are at Christmas. I first heard the potatoes grumbling about this years ago. What's that? Oh, yes, potatoes can talk. I probably shouldn't be telling you this but when you are asleep, all the fruits and vegetables and canned goods and dishes and silverware and whatnot in the kitchen get up and sing and dance. Over the years some pretty good singing groups have gotten their start in the kitchen. Let's see, there were The Platters, Canned Heat, The Lovin' Spoonful, and the spiritual group called Lettuce Pray.

Anyway, the kitchen clan wanted the potatoes to teach everyone that old dance, "The Mashed Potato".

The potatoes were pleased to teach. They'd hop up on the counter and lead us through the steps. Everyone seemed to finally get it except the bananas; when they danced they'd get so hot that they had to peel off their skins. You guessed it, they kept slipping on them.

But last Christmas, this all changed. The potatoes refused to teach, talk, dance, sing, do anything. Everyone wondered why.

The week before Christmas, Alice the Apple finally spoke for the rest of the kitchen.

ALICE THE APPLE: Potatoes, please tell us what's wrong. This is not like you, and we all want you to share in our Christmas celebration again this year.

CHRISTOPHER: At first the potatoes said nothing. Just sat there until that wiseacre Walter the Waffle Maker said:

WALTER THE WAFFLE MAKER: What's the matter potatoes, got a chip on your shoulder? Get it, chip? Ha, ha!

ALICE THE APPLE: That'll be enough Walter. C'mon potatoes, please tell us what's wrong.

CHRISTOPHER: After a pause, Penelope the Potato spoke up.

PENELOPE THE POTATO: Well, if you must know, we potatoes feel neglected at Christmastime. We feel taken for granted.

WALTER THE WAFFLE MAKER: Kinda feel like . . . small potatoes, do you? Ha, ha! Oh, that's good, that goooood.

ALICE THE APPLE: Walter, please!

PENELOPE THE POTATO: Oh, sure. Make fun of us potatoes. But let me tell you, we feed this family throughout the year, day-in, day-out. We can be baked, boiled, fried, scalloped, au gratined, even mashed—we don't care. Just happy to serve. But when Christmas comes and everyone puts out their best dishes and has parties and family gatherings, we get overlooked.

ALICE THE APPLE: But Penelope, you're there for every Christmas dinner. What would the turkey or ham—or certainly, lutefisk—be without your helping?

WALTER THE WAFFLE MAKER: Or without a helping of you?

PENELOPE THE POTATO: But who do the dinner guests talk about? Tom Turkey and Lena the Lutefisk—everyone but us. Even Chester the Chestnut gets more attention, and people eat chestnuts maybe once a year! For goodness' sake, songs are written with chestnuts in the lyrics, but have you ever heard a Christmas song with the words, "Potatoes roasting on the open fire"?

CHRISTOPHER: Everyone went silent. No one had ever thought about it that way, that certain foods get all the attention at Christmastime.

This conversation was making the cranberries rather uneasy. Now, don't get me wrong. I like cranberries. Some of my best friends are cranberries. But they have an . . . air about them. Cranberries think they are something special simply because people insist on cranberries in their Christmas dinner. Sometime I'd like to tell cranberries that the only reason they're included is that people like putting something red on the table and they know catsup's too tacky.

Anyway, no one said anything until Clarisse the Cranberry spoke.

CLARISSE THE CRANBERRY: Penelope, I had no idea you felt this way. But Penelope, dear, you have to admit that there is a reason for it all. I mean, you're . . . you're plain, to put it bluntly. You're not much to look at, with all those eyes and such.

However, looks aren't everything. Look at the raisins. Poor dears, all wrinkled and shriveled. Yet they do all right for themselves, and Lord knows they've been nearly impossible to live with since their California raisins TV commercial success. If I hear that song, "Heard It Through the Grapevine" one more time, I'll die.

So looks aren't everything. The secret, especially at Christmastime, is to be sweet. You? You simply have no taste. That's why they cover you with gravy. I'd rather not be the one to tell you, but do you know why the children of the house don't like you? You're not sweet.

CHRISTOPHER: That hurt. The potatoes adored the children—Ben, Nathan, Brianna, and Kate—but the kids seemed indifferent to potatoes.

Much as I hate to admit it, Clarisse had a point. Christmas is a time of sweets with all the fudge and candy canes and cookies and peanut brittle and fruit cakes.

Poor Penelope couldn't say much. It was getting on toward morning, and everyone started to go back to their places before the people of the house got up.

The next night, which was the night before Christmas, the kitchen clan had its Christmas party—dancing and caroling and carrying on. Of course, they had to make sure they didn't disturb the glass of chocolate milk and the plate of cookies that Ben, Brianna, Nathan, and Kate had set out on the kitchen table for Santa Claus. There was also a note:

Dear Santa Claus,

Here are some goodies for you because you work hard. Got an idea for you. You can lighten your load and not work so hard if you leave more presents here.

Your pals,
Ben, Kate, Nathan, and Brianna

I said that all of the kitchen clan were partying. Not quite all. The potatoes had been huddled up and were whispering excitedly. Then all of a sudden they walked over to the cupboard and pulled out a pan. They put chocolate and butter in it and turned on the stove. Finally, Alice the Apple just had to ask.

ALICE THE APPLE: Penelope, what are you potatoes up to?

PENELOPE THE POTATO: Well, we potatoes got to thinking about what Clarisse the Cranberry said. About sweetness? I must admit she made some sense. So we figure that if sweetness is what it takes to get attention at Christmastime, then we'll go sweet.

CLARISSE THE CRANBERRY: You don't mean that you're going to become chocolate-covered potatoes?

PENELOPE THE POTATO: You got it. We're going to surprise Santa Claus.

CLARISSE THE CRANBERRY: You'll also be the laughing stock of the kitchen. Penelope, you're being ridiculous.

PENELOPE THE POTATO: Oh, cram it, you old cranberry. You're just jealous.

CHRISTOPER: We all were in shock as several potatoes, one by one, plopped into the melted chocolate and butter. Then, one by one, they climbed out and marched from the stove to the kitchen table. There they lined up in two rows just above the note from Ben, Nathan, Brianna, and Kate.

And just in time because at that moment we all heard a clump-clump-clump on the roof. Was it Santa Claus? I heard noise in the back yard and then saw Santa with his reindeer. Santa liked to let his reindeer stretch their legs once in a while, and I could see the red glow of Rudolf the Red-Nosed Reindeer as he sniffed around the garden.

I could hear Santa climbing back on the roof, and then slide down the chimney. I heard him grunt and groan as he crawled out of the fireplace. He coughed and dusted himself off. Then I heard footsteps as he made his way to the kitchen. Suddenly, I saw his great white beard and red hat pop through the doorway, and everyone shouted, "Hi Santa!" Santa smiled and said:

SANTA CLAUS: Ho, ho, ho. Merry Christmas! It so nice to see you all again.

CHRISTOPHER: He walked across the kitchen, looked at me and said "Hi." It's a little tradition he started when he noticed the dancing Santa on my grandfather, Christopher the Christmas Pot Holder I. He's said "Hi" every year since. I asked him how his reindeer were.

SANTA CLAUS: Oh, they're about the same. All but Dancer and Prancer. This year they are wearing leg warmers.

CHRISTOPHER: Because of the cold? I asked.

SANTA CLAUS: No, no. They are into aerobics. The elves back at the North Pole call them Aerobic Dancer and Aerobic Prancer.

CHRISTOPHER: Santa chuckled, then read the note from Ben, Nathan, Brianna, and Kate. He chuckled again. His eyes widened as he spied the chocolate milk and cookies, and he said:

SANTA CLAUS: Now wasn't that nice of those kids to leave me this. But you know, I'm all sweeted out. Everywhere I go I get sweets, and too many sweets aren't good for old Santa. Just once I wish someone would leave me something substantial. Hello, what do we have here?

CHRISTOPHER: Santa reached in his pocket and put on his glasses. Then he picked up a chocolate-covered potato. He frowned, then went to open the kitchen window. He called for Rudolf the Red-Nosed Reindeer, and in a moment Rudolf stuck his antlers and then his beaming red nose through the window. The whole room took on a red glow.

SANTA CLAUS: Rudolf, what do you make of this little item?

CHRISTOPHER: Rudolf sniffed the chocolate-covered potato and got a little chocolate on his red nose. He licked the chocolate off and, in disapproval, started shaking his head. Then he said:

RUDOLF THE RED-NOSED REINDEER: Santa, for some odd reason someone, perhaps with a poor sense of humor, has taken a perfectly good potato and yukked it up with chocolate.

CHRISTOPHER: Santa raised his eyebrows for a moment, then proceeded to wipe the chocolate off all the potatoes. He sat in a chair, leaned back, and asked for an explanation. The potatoes kinda fidgeted. I swear the Idaho whites were so embarrassed they suddenly turned into North Dakota reds. Finally Penelope the Potato spoke up.

PENELOPE THE POTATO: Well Santa, it's like this. We just wanted some attention at Christmastime. It seems that only sweet things get attention, so we decided . . .

SANTA CLAUS: To cover yourself with chocolate? I see . . . Look, Penelope and all you potatoes, you're fine just the way you are. You don't need chocolate or anything else. You're great. Now, I've got an idea.

CHRISTOPER: The potatoes were thrilled by what Santa had said. Suddenly, Santa jumped up out of his seat and reached for pans and bowls and potatoes. I won't tell you exactly what Santa did or how he did it. That's a secret.

But I will tell you that Santa finished in the kitchen and left gifts. Then he wished us a merry Christmas and left. I could hear the reindeer harnessing up on the roof, and a moment later after takeoff I saw the sleigh and Rudolf's red nose high in the sky.

Then, because Santa likes the kitchen clan I guess, he guided his sleigh back toward us, flying low and coming right down the middle of the street. Santa turned the sleigh sharply and it whooshed by our window so close that we could hear the reindeer panting as they pulled. After a sharp climb, Santa gave a final wave and was off until next year.

Early Christmas morning, I heard little feet shuffling upstairs. It was Ben, Nathan, Brianna, and Kate. They raced down the stairs and screamed and giggled at the gifts. They couldn't wait for their parents to get up. Then one of them wondered out loud if Santa had eaten the cookies and chocolate milk.

They flew into the kitchen and were in wonder to see that the plate and the glass were empty. But what was this? In the center of the table was a stack of lefse, which the kids loved, and a note from Santa:

Dear Ben, Nathan, Brianna, and Kate,

Made these rounds of lefse especially for you out of potatoes, one of my favorite foods. Merry Christmas.

Santa

How to
Make Lefse

I REMEMBER putting down a hardwood floor in my bedroom. I planned and planned and double-checked every detail. I also avoided putting down that first strip of wood.

Finally, after a couple more hours of avoidance, my six-year-old son, Ben, came in and asked, "What you doing, Dad?"

I barely heard him, so immersed was I in thought. "Uh, I'm putting a floor down, Ben."

"How do you do it?"

"Well, you put the glue on the floor with this"—I showed Ben the trowel—"and then you put these wood strips on the glue."

"That's it? Sounds fun."

"Uh-huh." I was again far away in thought.

Ben waited a moment, gave me a look, and finally said, "So, what's you *doing*, Dad?"

With learning to make lefse, you have to prepare and think about equipment, recipes, and technique. But ultimately you have to start doing; you have to start rolling and grilling and making mistakes. If the whole process doesn't re-

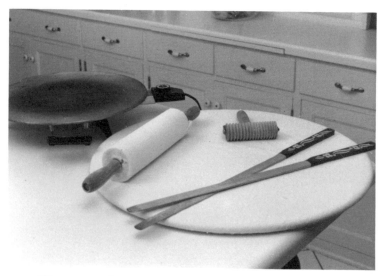

What you need to get you going. You can make lefse with less, but the electric grill, the rollers, sticks, and cloth-covered pastry board sure make lefse making slick. (Photos in this "How To" section by Darroll Bengtson.)

main fun and satisfying, then try lefse making with others. If it's still not fun, then forget it.

Making a mess is a major reason many folks forget it. You are going to get flour all over the place, even after you're an old pro. I've learned to live with it by practicing my old soft shoe while the floor is floury ("Tea for two, and me for you . . .").

But if you can't stand the mess in your kitchen, try setting up your lefse-making plant in the basement. One of the best lefse makers I know, Bitten Norvoll in Minneapolis, has her rolling board and grill atop a board atop her washer and dryer in the basement.

So let's give it a go, here. To start, purchase the right equipment. Yes, you can get by with substitutes, but give yourself some early Christmas presents; go to a Scandinavi-an shop and buy a sixteen-inch grill, one or two twenty-four-inch lefse sticks with beveled tips, a cotton-polyester pastry cloth, and a grooved rolling pin, which reduces sticking es-pecially when covered by a cotton-polyester sock.

If you don't want to spend a lot of money on lefse making right away, you can probably get by with what you have in your house now. Kathy Weflen, in St. Paul, started making lefse using a cast iron skillet instead of a lefse grill. She couldn't grill the really big rounds, but when starting out you should make more manageable rounds anyway. Weflen also used a spatula instead of a lefse stick. Simple tools, she said, but "I had nothing to lose. If the lefse didn't turn out, I had an excuse."

Ethel Olson, Olga Evenmoe, Mabel Holten, and Inez Wilhelmson of Spring Grove, Minnesota, suggested several substitutes for lefse sticks. You can sand down part of a peach crate, or just use the long sticks in window shades and shave down one end to a point.

You don't need to buy a round board for rolling, with its own custom fitted pastry cloth. Just put the backside of an oilcloth, or a simple dish towel, on the counter top. Edna and Palmer Bergsgaard of Spring Grove for years have just used a $2 \times 3'$ sheet of ½-inch plywood covered with oilcloth wrong side up.

A lefse rolling pin, grooved or with miniature pyramids on it, is the hardest piece of equipment to substitute for. You can use a smooth pin covered with a sock, as Ida Sacquitne of Decorah, Iowa, does, to roll out thin lefse. But she finishes her rounds with a lefse pin. So if you only want to spend money on one lefse-making piece of equipment, make it the pin. Some pins have handles fixed to the rolling area, others don't. Your choice. The fixed handles get nice and smooth, and this type of pin is quieter in the long run because there are no moving—and squeaking—parts.

One last equipment item: Socks are sold for rolling pins, and they aren't expensive. Some lefse makers don't like them because they absorb flour which can get into the dough and make it tough. Other lefse makers love socks because they prevent dough, especially dough rich with butter and cream and therefore slightly sticky, from sticking to the pin. I like a sock, but I didn't buy one. I just slipped an old cotton-polyester athletic sock over my lefse pin. I cut a hole in the toe for one handle and thumb-tacked the other end of the sock around the other handle. Crude but effective. (I did wash the sock first.)

And now for the steps involved in making lefse. There is no right way to make lefse, except a way that works. And the only wrong way is the way that doesn't work. (Absolutely brilliant, huh?) So, that means there's a lot of leeway in making potato lefse.

Step 1: Boil Potatoes. Boil Russet potatoes, which are dry potatoes, until they are soft. Don't boil them too long. Once they go mushy, they have absorbed too much water. This means you'll have to add more flour later, which toughens and dries the lefse.

I peel my potatoes before boiling. It's kind of boring, at times, but my son, Ben, and I made up a little tune to sing while peeling. Sing it to the tune of the old gospel hymn, "Steal Away":

> Peel away, peel away
> Peel away the taters.
> Peel away, peel away home.
> We ain't got long till lefse.

I may change my peeling ways, however, after talking with a couple lefse makers. Kathy Weflen said that many of a potato's nutrients are in, or right below, the skin. Therefore, she's made lefse with skins and all in it. "People kinda look at the lefse strange," she said, but these lefse are just as tasty, and are more nutritious.

Bitten Norvoll also boils potatoes with the skins on. She said potatoes absorb less water that way. She skins her boiled spuds, though, by picking off just the thin peel. That way nutrients right below the skin are retained.

Step 2: Drain Potatoes. Drain as much water off as you can. Elida Peterson of Rushford, Minnesota, drains hers in a colander.

Isn't that "rice" that two siblings, son Ben and daughter Kate, can get along long enough to help out with ricing the potatoes?

Step 3: Mash and Rice Potatoes. Mash the potatoes while they are still warm. Then rice the mashed potatoes once or twice to get out the lumps.

Step 4: Cool Potatoes. Until this step, there is little disagreement. And all lefse makers say you should let your potatoes cool; cooled dough needs less flour to roll out. Less flour means lefse that's less tough and dry.

Ben adding the shortening to the potatoes. My recipe calls for melted margarine and butter.

The question is: How cool? I do my potatoes and then cover and cool them overnight in the refrigerator, or at least three or four hours. I have cooled my bowl of potatoes in a snowbank, but you need to keep an eye out for dogs. And don't put your bowl beneath where birds perch!

Herb and Anna Solum of Spring Grove put their potatoes in the garage to cool overnight. I like the garage idea in the winter; if there's a bad snowstorm and you need a little traction to get your car out, a handful of sticky lefse dough is right there for the pitching.

On the other hand, Eunice Stoen of Decorah and Elida Peterson wouldn't think of refrigerating their potatoes. Eunice said it's not necessary. Just cool the potatoes to room temperature and go onto the next step. And Elida said refrigerated potatoes "sweat," and anytime you have standing water around a batch of lefse you've got trouble. She let hers cool to room temperature, covering the bowl with a paper towel, so moisture can escape—so the dough can "breathe," as she put it.

Step 5: Add Shortening, Sugar, Salt, and Cream. Some lefse makers add all or some of these items (recipes vary) to riced potatoes before cooling, and some after. Kneading ingredients into the dough before cooling allows flavors to mix thoroughly, making for a little better taste; adding after cooling and shortly before adding flour and rolling keeps moisture out of the potatoes as long as possible.

Step 6: Knead Flour Into Dough. I add a little less flour than the recipe calls for. If the dough is still sticky, I add the rest of the flour called for. Keep in mind, you'll add flour later with rolling, so err on the side of less flour.

I feel kneady here. Sorry about that pun. (Not!)

Step 7: Keep Dough Cool. Keep your dough in the refrigerator while you roll and grill. Some lefse makers prefer at this stage to make dough balls about the size of an egg (¼ to ⅓ cup) and keep them refrigerated. While this may keep the dough drier, a cookie sheet of dough balls takes up space in the refrigerator and seems to be more bother than it's worth. I just pinch off ⅓ cup before rolling each round.

Step 8: Set Grill Temperature. Plug in your grill and set it at 500–550°.

Step 9: Roll. Bitten Norvoll said a common mistake among beginning rollers is "they try to make lefse too big." Don't try for a lefse that could pass for a kite, not your first time. Just roll out an eight- or ten-inch round.

Put flour on your pastry cloth and pin and start rolling. Eunice Stoen said, "If you start with your ball round, your lefse is more apt to stay round." On your first few passes with your roller, be gentle and wary of shape.

About a third of a cup makes a fourteen- to sixteen-inch lefse. Beginners should start with less dough and make eight- to ten-inch rounds. Notice the thumb tacks on my roller. I was too cheap to buy a fancy fitted lefse sock, so I used a cotton-polyester athletic sock (I did wash it first). I ran one handle through a hole in the toe and tacked the top of the sock to the other end of the roller.

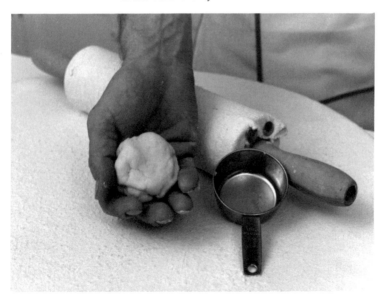

A little flour on the rolling pin prevents sticking.

A little flour on both sides of your lefse before rolling.

Start round to end round. That is, with the first few passes with your rolling pin, try to keep the shape round. If you don't, no big deal. You'll find that taste buds don't discriminate round from rhomboid.

Turn your round with a lefse stick at least once as you roll out the lefse. This helps prevent sticking.

After you have the round rolled out six or seven inches, slide your lefse stick underneath it and turn it over. Turning prevents sticking. Then finish rolling a nice thin round you can barely see through. If the round sticks, use your stick to slowly work the sticky spot free. The round may have a hole, which can be pinched together on the grill. If the lefse tears, re-roll with a bit more flour, but only after you've scraped off the sticky spot on your board or pin with a small knife.

Think about a rolling touch. The roller and the lefse are not enemies; one is not made to thump and pummel the other. I like Elida Peterson's approach to rolling. Elida has arthritis in her hips and cannot stand and lean her weight on the pin. She sits at her table and rolls, or rather, the *pin* does the rolling; her hands just guide the pin *across* the lefse, not down into it. She says less flour goes into the lefse that way.

Step 10: Put Lefse on Grill. I used to use two lefse sticks to transfer the round to the grill. I'd slip them under the rolled out lefse, lift it over to the grill, flop it down, and smooth it out. But peer pressure has gotten to me, so now I use the standard one-stick method. Lay your stick on an edge of the round. Using your fingernail or your other stick, flip the edge over the stick. Roll the stick toward the center of the lefse; this wraps the round around the stick. When the stick is near the center, pick up the lefse and put it on the grill by placing the dangling end on one side of the grill and unwrapping the lefse toward the other. The grill is hot, but you can still use fingers to slide the lefse into any position.

Step 11: Bake. Don't grill side one too long. Give it just a light singe (thirty-five to forty-five seconds), which causes bubbles to rise. Then flip the round while it still has most of its moisture for side two. Grill side two till the spots are the color you want. If you want, flip the round and touch up side one.

Once you have the lefse rolled out, you need to get it to the grill.
First flip an edge over a lefse stick.

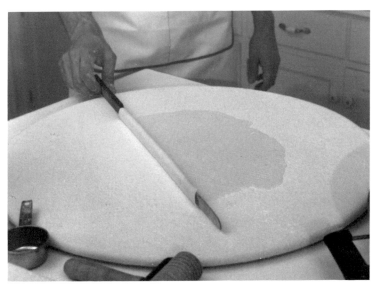

Rotate the stick to the center of the round.

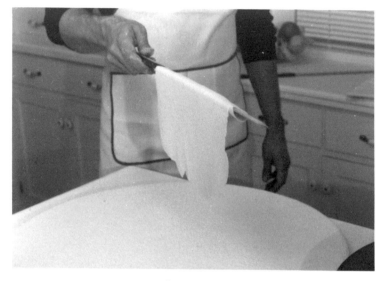

Lift and carry.

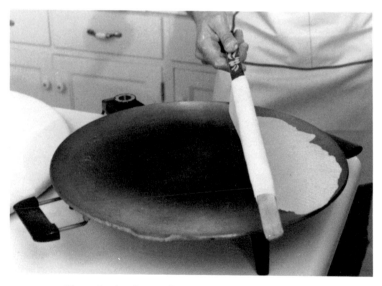

Place the dangling end on one side of the hot grill.

Rotate the stick to the other end of the grill . . .

. . . until the lefse is rolled out.

Grill until you see bubbles start to rise. Turn to do side two of the lefse, again until you see bubbles billow up. When in doubt, undercook. Chewy is better than crispy.

Done. Prepare to drool.

When I was at Norsland Kitchens in Rushford, I watched the baker closely. At first I thought she was careless with her stick when she flipped an edge up. I watched her do this several times, however, and realized she was saving that edge from drying out. The edge was done, but the center of the round wasn't yet.

Step 12: Cool, Stack, and Store. With a lefse stick remove your finished lefse from the grill and put it on a towel to cool. Cover with another towel to prevent drying. Ida Sacquitne told me how to stack lefse to soften the edges, which

Cool the lefse between towels. Let the round cool briefly, and then fold it in half and then in half again. Then stack this triangle with one ragged edge on other folded rounds. Make sure the straight edges always face out. This allows the ragged, sometimes drier edges to soften up in the moist interior of the stack. When stack has cooled, unfold each triangle before storing or freezing.

sometimes get crisp. Fold the finished rounds in half, and then fold them in half again. The folded rounds are triangular now and are stacked so the pointed corner and straight edges are always outside. The jagged third side is always inside and less exposed to the air. Since lefse will crease or stick together if left too long in this position, unfold them before refrigerating or freezing.

Plastic containers or double plastic bags keep lefse fresh in the fridge for a week or so. But Bitten Norvoll doesn't like the taste and texture of refrigerated lefse. She leaves hers out for only three days, or she freezes them. Lefse double-bagged in the freezer stays good for months. Elida Peterson places two or three unfolded rounds between wax paper. She seals the edges of the wax paper with her hot grill, and then puts the wax-papered lefse in a double plastic bag before freezing.

Step 13: Eat. The simplest of steps, really. Traditionally, people eat it plain; with butter; or with butter and sugar, brown sugar, or jam. Spread these ingredients on and roll, or fold, the lefse before eating. Some people put meats (lutefisk, ham, salmon, shrimp with sauce) cheeses, or fruits inside the roll.

In *91 Ways To Serve Lefse*, author Merlin Hoiness has come up with creative ways to eat lefse. When I was visiting Merlin in Rushford, I tasted this preparation called "Mr. Lefse's Original Party Hors d'oeuvres."

Layer 1: On a round of lefse spread eight ounces of Philadelphia cream cheese that has been mixed with three teaspoons of creamed horseradish.

Layer 2: On a round of lefse spread French onion dip and a little creamed horseradish. Lay out sliced boiled ham.

Layer 3: On a round of lefse spread French onion dip, sliced turkey breast, chopped ripe olives, and creamed horseradish.

Layer 4: On a round of lefse spread French onion dip, sliced dried beef, and creamed horseradish.

Layer 5: On a round of lefse spread Cheez Whiz, and sprinkle on ground walnuts.

Cut the layers of rounds into 1½-inch squares. Place a green olive on each square and spear both with a toothpick. Using twelve-inch lefse rounds, this makes about ninety hors d'oeuvres.

I found this poem in a book called *Cream and Bread*, by Janet Martin and Allen Todnem. As poems will do, it says what I've said about lefse making, but in just eight lines.

> Easy on the flour,
> Fast on the pace,
> Or the dough will stick
> All over the place.
>
> Roll 'em out thin,
> Fry 'em up quick;
> With butter and sugar
> They'll go down slick.

Recipes

E ACH LEFSE MAKER I talked with gave me his or her
recipe, which I now pass on to you. Most of the recipes
are similar, but if you try several or all, you might find
one more suited to your skills and tastes. Unless noted, I am
just listing the ingredients for potato lefse. Please refer to the
aforementioned how-to-make-lefse steps.

Eunice Stoen — Decorah, Iowa

5 c. riced potatoes
1 stick melted butter
3 T. powdered sugar
   (adds fluffiness, says Eunice)
2 c. flour
½ t. salt
Makes about 15 lefse, more or
   less depending on the size.

Euny cools her dough just to room temperature; she doesn't
refrigerate.

She says if you want to save on labor and use instant potatoes, don't go all instant. She doesn't like the taste. Instead, make one third of your potatoes using instant.

Lefse Kling

Euny says Lefse Kling is a Norwegian taco. With lefse as a base, put a handful of shredded lettuce on top, then browned ground beef, chopped tomatoes, chopped onions, cheese curds (put through food processor), and mild taco sauce. Fold ends and side and serve with two or three napkins. "Very tasty," she says, "but messy to eat."

Elida Peterson—Rushford, Minnesota

10 lb. potatoes, peeled, salted, cooked, and mashed.
   Mix with mashed potatoes the following:
½ pint of whipping cream
1 stick butter

Rice the potato-cream-butter mixture (about 16 cups), cover with paper towel, and cool on counter, not in refrigerator.
   After cooling, add ¾ c. flour to 3 c. of above mixture. Roll and grill this 3-cup batch, then add ¾ c. flour to another 3 c. of above mixture, roll and grill. Do this till potato mixture runs out. Keep extra mixture cool until rolling. Makes about 50 lefse.

Recipe for The World's Largest Lefse — Starbuck, Minnesota

30 lb. potatoes
35 lb. flour
1 lb. sugar
1 lb. powdered milk
4 lb. shortening (puff paste shortening, used by bakers.) Makes 1 lefse approximately 10-feet square.

Herb and Anna Solum — Spring Grove, Minnesota

To 4 c. riced potatoes add ¾ stick melted margarine and ⅓ c. whipping cream. Cool. When ready to roll add 2 t. sugar, 1 t. salt, and 1¼ c. flour. Makes about 12 lefse.

Bitten Norvoll—Minneapolis

5 c. riced potatoes
½ c. margarine
2 T. sugar
1 T. salt

Flour enough to be able to roll out thin. Makes about 15 lefse.

Potato Lefse with Instant Potatoes

Heat: 2⅔ c. water
⅓ c. milk
1 t. salt
5 T. butter

Remove from heat when ready to boil and stir in 2⅔ c. potato buds. Whip with fork until desired consistency. Chill. Work in 1½ c. flour or more until able to roll thin. Makes about 10 lefse.

Krinalefse

Mix: 3 eggs
¾ c. sugar
2 c. buttermilk or half sour cream
1 stick butter or margarine, melted
½ c. whipping cream
2 t. soda
1 T. lemon rind

Flour enough to be able to roll out thin. Design can be made on top with fork. Makes about 15 lefse.

Mix this filling and spread between two cooled rounds:
½ c. softened butter
¾ c. sugar
2-3 T. whipping cream
2 T. cardamom

Mør Lefse (Soft Lefse)

Mix together by hand the following:
2 c. sour cream
1 c. sugar
1 c. white corn syrup
1 c. butter, melted
2 eggs

Dissolve 2 t. (level) hartshorn powder (baking ammonia) in 1 T. lukewarm water, then add this to the first mixture. Enough flour to roll out, not too thin. Bake in oven at 450° for 8-10 minutes. Bake only on one side until very light and golden. Makes about 15 lefse.

Mix this filling and spread between two cooled rounds:
    ½ c. butter
    ¾ c. sugar
    2-3 T. whipping cream
    2 t. cinnamon

June Olson—Starbuck, Minnesota

Cook and mash 20 pounds of potatoes. Add 1 c. whipping cream, 2 sticks margarine (June says margarine browns better than butter) dash salt, and 1 T. sugar. Cool. Add 2 T. salad oil and then rice mixture. Enough flour to roll thin. Makes about 40 lefse.

Zola and Merlin Hoiness—Harmony, Minnesota

3 c. riced potatoes
3 T. pure vegetable shortening, melted
2 t. salt
1 c. flour
Makes about 10 lefse.

Sabel Jorde—Rushford, Minnesota

4 c. riced potatoes
¾ c. Crisco
2 T. salt
4 c. flour, less if you can.
Makes about 12 lefse.

Time for a musical break from trying recipes! Here are two songs about lefse. I found them at the end of Merlin Hoiness's book, *91 Ways To Serve Lefse*, but Merlin said he didn't know who wrote them. The first one is sung to the tune of "Deep in the Heart of Texas" and the second to "Deck the Halls."

"OH YA YOU BETCHA"

The lefse's round with spots of brown
Oh yah you betcha, uff da.
The lutefisk is such a risk
Oh yah you betcha, uff da.
The pickled herring is so daring
Oh yah you betcha, uff da.
My belly hurts from all those burps
Oh yah you betcha, uff da.

"DECK THE HALLS"

Deck the halls with lefse slices, fa la la la la la la uff da
Do not check on what the price is, fa la la la la la la uff da
Might be thought a strange creation, fa la la la la la la la la
But it's great as insulation, fa la la la la la la la uff da.

Lefse's sure to beat the fate-o, fa la la la la la la uff da
Of each old and cold potato, fa la la la la la la la uff da
Mix with lard, there's no waste, fa la la la la la la la la
Also notice there's no taste, fa la la la la la la la uff da.

Lefse is a Christmas treat, fa la la la la la la uff da
All the Scandinavians eat, fa la la la la la la uff da
Notice how the Norske flaunts it, fa la la la la la la la la
Even though nobody wants it, fa la la la la la la la uff da.

"Hard Lefse" — Story City, Iowa

3 c. milk
1 c. Crisco or lard
½ c. sugar
3 t. salt
8 c. flour

Heat milk and Crisco to rolling boil, dissolving Crisco. Measure sugar, salt, and flour into large bowl. Pour hot milk-Crisco liquid over dry ingredients a little at a time, mixing well. When cool enough to handle, add flour and knead. Make balls out of ¼ c. or ⅓ c. of dough and flatten on wax-paper lined tray. Cover with towel to keep balls warm.

Roll thin and bake on grill set at 350–450°. Fold in half the rounds, which harden and dry as they cool, and stack and cover with wax paper. Store in a cardboard box in a cool place. When ready to eat, dip half rounds into tray of water (120–125°.) Lift lefse out of water and let excess drip. To let soften, place lefse on towel and cover with wax paper for about 30 minutes. Serve as you would potato lefse. Makes about 30 lefse.

Olga Evenmoe and Mabel Holten (sisters) — Spring Grove, Minnesota

6 c. riced potatoes
2 sticks margarine
6 T. half & half
1 t. salt
3 c. flour
Makes about 15–20 lefse.

Ida Sacquitne — Decorah, Iowa

4 c. riced potatoes
Dash salt
Dash sugar
2–3 T. half & half
2 T. margarine
2 c. flour
Makes about 12 lefse.

Martha Mueller—Spring Grove, Minnesota

10 c. riced potatoes
1½ t. salt
1 stick margarine, melted. or 1/2 stick margarine and
    1/2 stick butter

Mix above ingredients. To 2½ c. of the above mixture, add
½ c. flour and 2 T. Carnation Milk. Repeat until potato-salt-
margarine mixture is gone. Roll and bake, says Martha, with
Handel's "Messiah" playing in the background. Makes about
30 lefse.

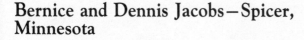

Bernice and Dennis Jacobs—Spicer, Minnesota

8 c. riced potatoes (25 to 30 medium-size potatoes)
¾ c. margarine, or lard, or butter
3 T. sugar
1 T. salt
2 c. flour
Makes about 25 lefse.

Jennie Legwold (my grandmother) — Peterson, Minnesota

2 c. riced potatoes
1 c. flour
6 T. margarine
2 T. carnation milk
Makes about 10 lefse.

Marie Kjome — Spring Grove, Minnesota

8 c. riced potatoes
1 c. butter
½ c. whipping cream
1 T. salt

Mix the above before potatoes cool. To 2 c. of this mixture add ⅔ c. flour. Roll and bake. Repeat until potato mixture is gone. Makes about 30 lefse.

Edna and Palmer Bergsgaard—Spring Grove, Minnesota

2 c. riced potatoes
1 T. lard
1 T. butter
1 T. whipping cream
1 t. salt
½ c. flour
Makes about 10 lefse.

John Glesne—Decorah, Iowa

4 c. riced potatoes
1 t. salt
¼ c. whipping cream
4 T. margarine
2 c. flour
Makes about 12 lefse.

Kathy Weflen — St. Paul

3 c. riced potatoes
3 T. shortening
3 T. whipping cream
1 T. salt
1 c. flour
Makes about 10 lefse.

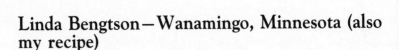

Linda Bengtson — Wanamingo, Minnesota (also my recipe)

3 c. riced potatoes (about 8 medium-size potatoes)
¼ c. melted margarine
1 T. melted butter
½ t. salt
1 T. sugar
¼ c. whipping cream
1¼ to 1½ c. flour
Makes about 10 lefse.

There are many, many other lefse recipes in Scandinavian cookbooks. But you have enough recipes here to keep you busy for an hour or two.

I'm going to leave you with two lefse songs (permission for use granted by the artists). The first one is "I'll Be Home For Lefse" by LeRoy Larson and The Minnesota Scandinavian Ensemble. The singer is pining for a good old-fashioned Scandinavian Christmas.

The second is probably the most famous lefse song of all time. It is the one and the only "Just A Little Lefse Will Go A Long Way" by Stan Boreson and Doug Setterberg.

"I'LL BE HOME FOR LEFSE"

I'll be home for lefse and the lutefisk.
You can put the rømmegrøt and rosettes on your list.
Christmas day you'll see me eating cheese and sylta
Lingonberries, Tom-and-Yerrys, peace on earth, good will.

I'll be home for lefse and the fattigmann.
You can bake a Christmas cake and flatbrød by the ton.
News Year's Eve you'll find me dancing at the hall
Valtz and schottische, polka, two-step, peace on earth to all.

"JUST A LITTLE LEFSE WILL GO A LONG WAY"

Lefse's good for many things, we can give you proof.
For tiling on the kitchen floor and patching up the roof.
Some people even use it as the soles upon their feet,
And some folks even think it's good to eat.

(chorus)

Just a little lefse will go a long way.
Gives you indigestion most all of the day.
Put it on your menu, you'll be sure to say
Just a little lefse will go a long way.

Leif Eriksson once had a boat, it was a leaky scow.
He said, "To beat Columbus we just got to leave right now."
The boat was leaking badly as they neared the U.S.A.
But he plugged the holes, yes, lefse saved the day.

(chorus)

Now if you know what lefse is then you can understood
It looks and feels like plastic and it tastes just like plywood.
We don't know what invented it, we don't know who's to
    blame
But if you are a Norske, you'll eat it just the same.

(chorus)